ADULT ACTIVITY BOOK

138 Pages in 6 categories

DOUGLAS DAViD

THIS ADULT ACTIVITY BOOK BELONGS TO:

Sudoku

Sudoku 1

				9	3	7	1	
9			7		6			
1							6	
			3			9		1
				8				
4		5			7			
	2							5
			2		8			4
	3	7	9	4				

Sudoku 2

9	3				2		4	
		7				8		
8	6				7			
		4					9	
			7		8			
	8					6		
			6				5	7
		5				1		
	4		9				8	6

Sudoku 3

	5	3		4			7	
						1		8
4				6				
		4	2	5		7		6
6		8		7	1	2		
				9				2
8		6						
	7			8		3	5	

Sudoku 4

		1		5				
	2	9	6	1				
4							1	
7					2	6		4
8								1
9		4	8					5
	5							3
				6	8	9	7	
				3		1		

Sudoku 5

	7						9	6
				5	7			4
9			6					1
	1						8	5
		5				6		
8	3						4	
3					2			8
4			8	9				
6	9						3	

Sudoku 6

9				5			6	8
5		7						
				6				4
4		3						
	1		2		7		8	
						2		3
7				1				
						1		6
3	5			4				2

Sudoku 7

2						9		
							7	8
		1	8			4		6
			6		8	5		
3				7				9
		9	5		4			
9		6			1	8		
7	1							
		8						5

Sudoku 8

		4	3					7
		7	8		5			4
6		8						
						6		3
	3		4		8		9	
1		2						
						8		6
7			2		6	9		
9					7	2		

Sudoku 9

		1		7		9		3
	4	9					5	
			2					
		2	9					5
8			5		6			4
5					2	3		
					8			
	8					2	3	
9		4		1		7		

Sudoku 10

3		1	8				6	
						8		
		9						3
	4		7	5	3		9	
9								1
	3		2	9	1		7	
4						6		
		6						
	8				7	3		4

Sudoku 11

				9			3	
8	5				3	2		
		7				6		
	8		2		4		9	1
1	2		3		8		5	
		4				9		
		3	9				8	4
	1			7				

Sudoku 12

1			5					
	6		9					7
9		2			1			8
			2	1			6	
		3				4		
	2			9	8			
2			7			5		3
7					9		2	
					5			9

Sudoku 13

				7	8			4
			5					
9		8			1	6		5
					2	7		1
		6				3		
1		4	9					
7		9	4			8		2
					9			
3			2	6				

Sudoku 14

4				6	3	5		
							9	3
			5			2		1
				5			4	
	7		3		9		8	
	2			8				
3		7			5			
6	5							
		8	1	2				5

Sudoku 15

6				7		8	9	
		5	2		8			3
	9				1			
			4					
7		1				9		4
					3			
			5				7	
8			1		2	6		
	4	9		3				2

Sudoku 16

8		7			2			
5		4			6			
		9	7					
3	6	5				1		
9								8
		8				3	5	6
					7	8		
			3			4		7
			8			2		3

Sudoku 17

			9			4		
8	2	4			3		6	
7					5		3	
							9	5
			2		8			
9	8							
	1		5					8
	6		7			1	2	4
		3			2			

Sudoku 18

	2	4			8			
				4		2		
9				5		7		
	7				9			2
		1	6		4	3		
6			3				7	
		3		6				7
		8		1				
			8			5	6	

Sudoku 19

	5		4			9		8
				1				
3			5		6			
	3	4		6				1
		6				5		
1				8		2	7	
			9		7			5
				4				
8		1			3		4	

Sudoku 20

					3	8	6	9
					2			
7	4						2	
8					7			2
		3		5		7		
2			8					1
	3						7	4
			1					
1	2	9	3					

Sudoku 21

7		1		8				9
	6	4				3		
8			1	3				
		9		4				
6								7
				5		6		
				7	5			1
		5				4	9	
9				6		7		3

Sudoku 22

			7			3		
6	5		2				9	
		4	8					2
		6	5			2	1	
	7	5			6	8		
7					5	1		
	9				2		6	3
		8			3			

Sudoku 23

					3			
3	6	7		4				8
			8	6				
		6	5					2
9	4						5	3
8					1	7		
				7	2			
6				8		1	3	7
			4					

Sudoku 24

	2				3		1	8
				1		5		
		9			2			
		3	1	4	9			6
7			2	6	5	8		
			8			1		
		6		7				
2	7		9				3	

Sudoku 25

	7							
		5		9				
9		8	1				7	
	6		2					4
		2	6	5	1	7		
7					8		3	
	4				3	5		6
				2		8		
							1	

Sudoku 26

		1					7	5
			4					
	8		6	3				
8						2	9	
5		7	8		9	4		1
	9	6						8
				1	5		3	
					8			
9	5					7		

Sudoku 27

1		8			3			
							4	
	6		4	2		5		3
3			2		1		8	
	8		6		9			2
2		7		3	4		9	
	9							
			7			2		8

Sudoku 28

2	9				4			
1			6				4	
		7						
4		8			2	9		6
			7		9			
9		3	5			2		1
						3		
	2				7			5
			1				2	9

Sudoku 29

4		9		7		2		1
	3	5	4					
								7
		2	3		5			6
8			7		6	1		
9								
					3	4	8	
6		1		9		3		5

Sudoku 30

					7	6		5
		5	4		6		7	9
				1			3	
		1						
	5	8				1	6	
						2		
	2			4				
6	1		9		8	3		
9		7	3					

Tubular Mazes

Tubular Maze 1

Tubular Maze 2

Tubular Maze 3

Tubular Maze 4

Tubular Maze 5

Tubular Maze 6

Tubular Maze 7

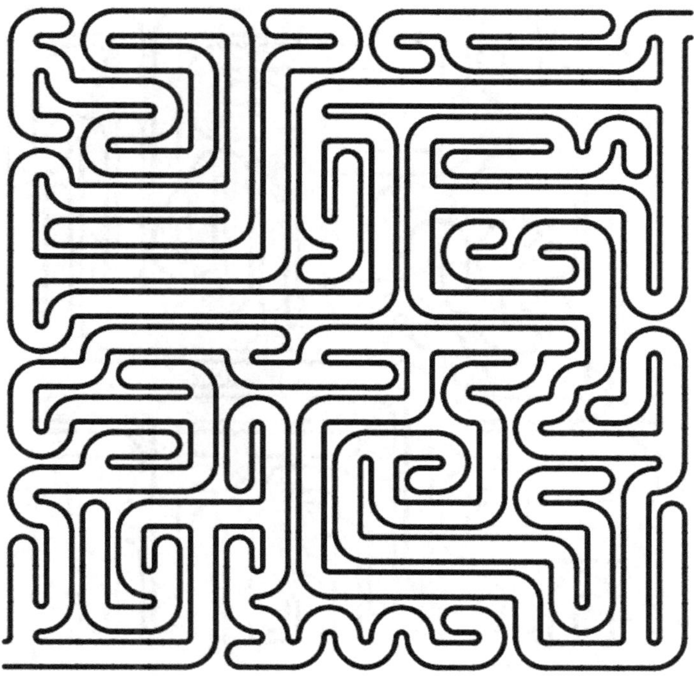

Tubular Maze 8

Tubular Maze 9

Tubular Maze 10

Tubular Maze 11

Tubular Maze 12

Tubular Maze 13

Tubular Maze 14

Tubular Maze 15

Tubular Maze 16

Tubular Maze 17

Tubular Maze 18

Tubular Maze 19

Tubular Maze 20

Tubular Maze 21

Tubular Maze 22

Tubular Maze 23

Tubular Maze 24

Tubular Maze 25

Tubular Maze 26

Tubular Maze 27

Tubular Maze 28

Tubular Maze 29

Tubular Maze 30

Word Scramble

Word Scramble List 1

Scrambled	Answer
C L S E P A I	S _ _ _ _ _ _
L U E Y	Y _ _ _
C P N R E E A P A A	A _ _ _ _ _ _ _ _ _
A L O R C L	C _ _ _ _ _
L H I S L	H _ _ _ _
A N S A T	S _ _ _ _
N W T O	T _ _ _
L E M	E _ _
C O R E J I E	R _ _ _ _ _ _
I O P E T T	T _ _ _ _ _

Word Scramble List 2

Scrambled	Answer
L Y U E	Y _ _ _
E P A A P R C N E A	A _ _ _ _ _ _ _ _ _
A C O L R L	C _ _ _ _ _
S I H L L	H _ _ _ _
A A T S N	S _ _ _ _
O N W T	T _ _ _
E M L	E _ _
E I C O E R J	R _ _ _ _ _ _
I E T P O T	T _ _ _ _ _
C E O R D	D _ _ _ _

Word Scramble List 3

Scrambled	Answer
P A R P E C E A N A	A _ _ _ _ _ _ _ _ _
L L C O A R	C _ _ _ _ _
H S L I L	H _ _ _ _
T S A A N	S _ _ _ _
O N W T	T _ _ _
M L E	E _ _
R O E I J E C	R _ _ _ _ _ _
T E P I T O	T _ _ _ _ _
R D C E O	D _ _ _ _
E R T V O A C O	O _ _ _ _ _ _ _

Word Scramble List 4

Scrambled	Answer
L A R C O L	C _ _ _ _ _
I S L H L	H _ _ _ _
A T N S A	S _ _ _ _
N W O T	T _ _ _
E L M	E _ _
J R C E E I O	R _ _ _ _ _ _
P T E I O T	T _ _ _ _ _
R O C E D	D _ _ _ _
A R E C T O O V	O _ _ _ _ _ _ _
O N E S	N _ _ _

Word Scramble List 5

I L L H S	H
T A N S A	S
N T W O	T
E M L	E
E I E J R O C	R
P T I O E T	T
D R E C O	D
R E O A O V T C	O
N O S E	N
E C I O E P N N	P

Word Scramble List 6

T S A A N	S
N O W T	T
E M L	E
I C O R E E J	R
O T I E T P	T
O D C E R	D
V O R E O A C T	O
S N O E	N
P N E N C E O I	P
U E F S F T R	S

Word Scramble List 7

Scrambled	Answer
N T WO	T _ _ _
M L E	E _ _
C O E J I E R	R _ _ _ _ _ _
T P T O E I	T _ _ _ _ _
C D R O E	D _ _ _ _
C E A R O T V O	O _ _ _ _ _ _ _
E O S N	N _ _ _
C P O N E I N E	P _ _ _ _ _ _ _
F F S R T U E	S _ _ _ _ _ _
I D Y L T E E U	Y _ _ _ _ _ _ _

Word Scramble List 8

Scrambled	Answer
E M L	E _ _
E E R J I O C	R _ _ _ _ _ _
O P T E T I	T _ _ _ _ _
R C O E D	D _ _ _ _
V T C O E O A R	O _ _ _ _ _ _ _
E S N O	N _ _ _
I N C E O E N P	P _ _ _ _ _ _ _
U F F E T S R	S _ _ _ _ _ _
U E L Y T I E D	Y _ _ _ _ _ _ _
O C O C A	C _ _ _ _

Word Scramble List 9

E E C O R I J	R
T E I P O T	T
C D O R E	D
O C O E A R T V	O
N E O S	N
N N C E I E O P	P
U F R S E F T	S
E E U Y T I D L	Y
C O C A O	C
A R O V I S	S

Word Scramble List 10

T I P E T O	T
R O C D E	D
T E O C R O A V	O
S E N O	N
I C N E N P E O	P
S T F U F E R	S
E Y L U D I T E	Y
O A O C C	C
S I A V O R	S
O E C U D L I S I	D

Word Scramble List 11

Scrambled	Answer
E C R D O	D _ _ _ _
A V O T O R E C	O _ _ _ _ _ _ _
S O N E	N _ _ _
E N C E I N P O	P _ _ _ _ _ _ _
T E F S R F U	S _ _ _ _ _ _
Y L D U T I E E	Y _ _ _ _ _ _ _
C A O O C	C _ _ _ _
O I S R V A	S _ _ _ _ _
E C I O L S I U D	D _ _ _ _ _ _ _ _
E E R E E M R D	R _ _ _ _ _ _ _

Word Scramble List 12

Scrambled	Answer
O C O A E T V R	O _ _ _ _ _ _ _
N E S O	N _ _ _
O N C N P E I E	P _ _ _ _ _ _ _
F R F S E T U	S _ _ _ _ _ _
T D U I E E Y L	Y _ _ _ _ _ _ _
A O O C C	C _ _ _ _
V A R O I S	S _ _ _ _ _
I L U C E D O S I	D _ _ _ _ _ _ _ _
M R E R E E D E	R _ _ _ _ _ _ _
O P E L	P _ _ _

Word Scramble List 13

O E N S	N
N C O E E N P I	P
U S F E F T R	S
E L E D Y U I T	Y
O C C A O	C
S A R V I O	S
I U L I E D S C O	D
D E M E E R R E	R
P L O E	P
G T F I	G

Word Scramble List 14

C O N I N P E E	P
F S R F T E U	S
T L E U D Y I E	Y
O O A C C	C
A O I V R S	S
I O D E C I L S U	D
E R E M E E D R	R
O L P E	P
G I F T	G
S O B T O	B

Word Scramble List 15

Scrambled	Answer
E S R T U F F	S _ _ _ _ _ _
L E D Y T U I E	Y _ _ _ _ _ _ _
C O C O A	C _ _ _ _
S O R A V I	S _ _ _ _ _
E L I U C O I D S	D _ _ _ _ _ _ _ _
E E E R E D M R	R _ _ _ _ _ _ _
P L O E	P _ _ _
I G F T	G _ _ _
S T O B O	B _ _ _ _
I L S R E V	S _ _ _ _ _

Word Scramble List 16

Scrambled	Answer
L E T U Y E I D	Y _ _ _ _ _ _ _
A C C O O	C _ _ _ _
R A S O I V	S _ _ _ _ _
I E I O D L U S C	D _ _ _ _ _ _ _ _
D M R E E R E E	R _ _ _ _ _ _ _
O P E L	P _ _ _
G T F I	G _ _ _
O B O S T	B _ _ _ _
I L E S R V	S _ _ _ _ _
C A K S	S _ _ _

Word Scramble List 17

O O C C A	C _ _ _ _
O V A S I R	S _ _ _ _ _
E U O C I S L I D	D _ _ _ _ _ _ _ _
R E E E R D M E	R _ _ _ _ _ _ _
L E O P	P _ _ _
F I T G	G _ _ _
S T O B O	B _ _ _ _
I E R S V L	S _ _ _ _ _
A S C K	S _ _ _
E I V G	G _ _ _

Word Scramble List 18

O A I R V S	S _ _ _ _ _
E L O I C D S U I	D _ _ _ _ _ _ _ _
M E D E R E E R	R _ _ _ _ _ _ _
L O E P	P _ _ _
T F I G	G _ _ _
O T O S B	B _ _ _ _
S R L E V I	S _ _ _ _ _
S K A C	S _ _ _
V I E G	G _ _ _
F M R E A	F _ _ _ _

Word Scramble List 19

S E I U D I C L O	D
R E E D E M E R	R
E O P L	P
I F G T	G
B O O S T	B
L V S E I R	S
K A S C	S
I E V G	G
F E M A R	F
R A I F A D	A

Word Scramble List 20

M E E E R R E D	R
O L E P	P
T I F G	G
S B T O O	B
S I V R L E	S
A S C K	S
V G I E	G
E F R A M	F
F I A D A R	A
E C R E C H	C

Word Scramble List 21

P O E L	P _ _ _
T I F G	G _ _ _
O S O B T	B _ _ _ _
R E S V I L	S _ _ _ _ _
S C K A	S _ _ _
V G E I	G _ _ _
M A F E R	F _ _ _ _
D R F A I A	A _ _ _ _ _
E C H E C R	C _ _ _ _ _
F U K A R E C T I	F _ _ _ _ _ _ _ _

Word Scramble List 22

G I T F	G _ _ _
B T O S O	B _ _ _ _
S L I V E R	S _ _ _ _ _
A C S K	S _ _ _
I E V G	G _ _ _
F A M R E	F _ _ _ _
A R I D F A	A _ _ _ _ _
R E C E C H	C _ _ _ _ _
A U I K F T E C R	F _ _ _ _ _ _ _ _
A L F E A R B T D	F _ _ _ _ _ _ _ _

Word Scramble List 23

Scrambled	Answer
S O T O B	B _ _ _ _
E S L I V R	S _ _ _ _ _
S A K C	S _ _ _
E G V I	G _ _ _
R F M E A	F _ _ _ _
A D R A I F	A _ _ _ _ _
H E E C C R	C _ _ _ _ _
T A C E I R U F K	F _ _ _ _ _ _ _ _
R D A F E A B T L	F _ _ _ _ _ _ _ _
S C O K	S _ _ _

Word Scramble List 24

Scrambled	Answer
S L I R E V	S _ _ _ _ _
S C K A	S _ _ _
E V G I	G _ _ _
A M R E F	F _ _ _ _
A D I A R F	A _ _ _ _ _
C R E E H C	C _ _ _ _ _
R A I U K C F T E	F _ _ _ _ _ _ _ _
A D R L B E A F T	F _ _ _ _ _ _ _ _
C K S O	S _ _ _
U I O G E S I R L	R _ _ _ _ _ _ _ _

Word Scramble List 25

Scrambled	Answer
A K S C	S _ _ _
I E V G	G _ _ _
M E F A R	F _ _ _ _
R A I A D F	A _ _ _ _ _
E R C H C E	C _ _ _ _ _
E F R I C T K U A	F _ _ _ _ _ _ _ _
L T E A B D F R A	F _ _ _ _ _ _ _ _
K C S O	S _ _ _
R I E S G L I U O	R _ _ _ _ _ _ _ _
D S O U N	S _ _ _ _

Word Scramble List 26

Scrambled	Answer
E V G I	G _ _ _
A F E R M	F _ _ _ _
D A I R A F	A _ _ _ _ _
E H C R C E	C _ _ _ _ _
I E K A C U T F R	F _ _ _ _ _ _ _ _
D F A R L A E B T	F _ _ _ _ _ _ _ _
K C S O	S _ _ _
E L G O R I I S U	R _ _ _ _ _ _ _ _
D U S N O	S _ _ _ _
I R V E E S C	S _ _ _ _ _ _

Word Scramble List 27

Scrambled	Answer
E F A M R	F _ _ _ _
I R A D F A	A _ _ _ _ _
H C E E R C	C _ _ _ _ _
U F C K R T E A I	F _ _ _ _ _ _ _ _
L F A E D B A T R	F _ _ _ _ _ _ _ _
S C K O	S _ _ _
I I L R G E U S O	R _ _ _ _ _ _ _ _
U D O N S	S _ _ _ _
C I V S E E R	S _ _ _ _ _ _
E C N O G I R I J	R _ _ _ _ _ _ _ _

Word Scramble List 28

Scrambled	Answer
F D A A R I	A _ _ _ _ _
C E R E H C	C _ _ _ _ _
R T A U E I C F K	F _ _ _ _ _ _ _ _
F L A B D T E A R	F _ _ _ _ _ _ _ _
O K C S	S _ _ _
I R L E G S O U I	R _ _ _ _ _ _ _ _
N U O D S	S _ _ _ _
C E E S I R V	S _ _ _ _ _ _
O J R C G E I N I	R _ _ _ _ _ _ _ _
N O G L E G I B N	B _ _ _ _ _ _ _ _

Word Scramble List 29

C R H E C E	C _ _ _ _ _
T U I C A E K F R	F _ _ _ _ _ _ _ _
L R E D B A F A T	F _ _ _ _ _ _ _ _
S C K O	S _ _ _
S E R U O L I G I	R _ _ _ _ _ _ _ _
O D U N S	S _ _ _ _
S V R C E E I	S _ _ _ _ _ _
O E J I G C R N I	R _ _ _ _ _ _ _ _
I G L B O E G N N	B _ _ _ _ _ _ _ _
M E E N T E C T X I	E _ _ _ _ _ _ _ _ _

Word Scramble List 30

A K F U C E I R T	F _ _ _ _ _ _ _ _
A T R D B E L F A	F _ _ _ _ _ _ _ _
K O C S	S _ _ _
O S U I E I R G L	R _ _ _ _ _ _ _ _
U N S O D	S _ _ _ _
C R E S E V I	S _ _ _ _ _ _
G J C E R N O I I	R _ _ _ _ _ _ _ _
G I E O N N L G B	B _ _ _ _ _ _ _ _
E E N T T M X I C E	E _ _ _ _ _ _ _ _ _
U O S L	S _ _ _

Colortile

1

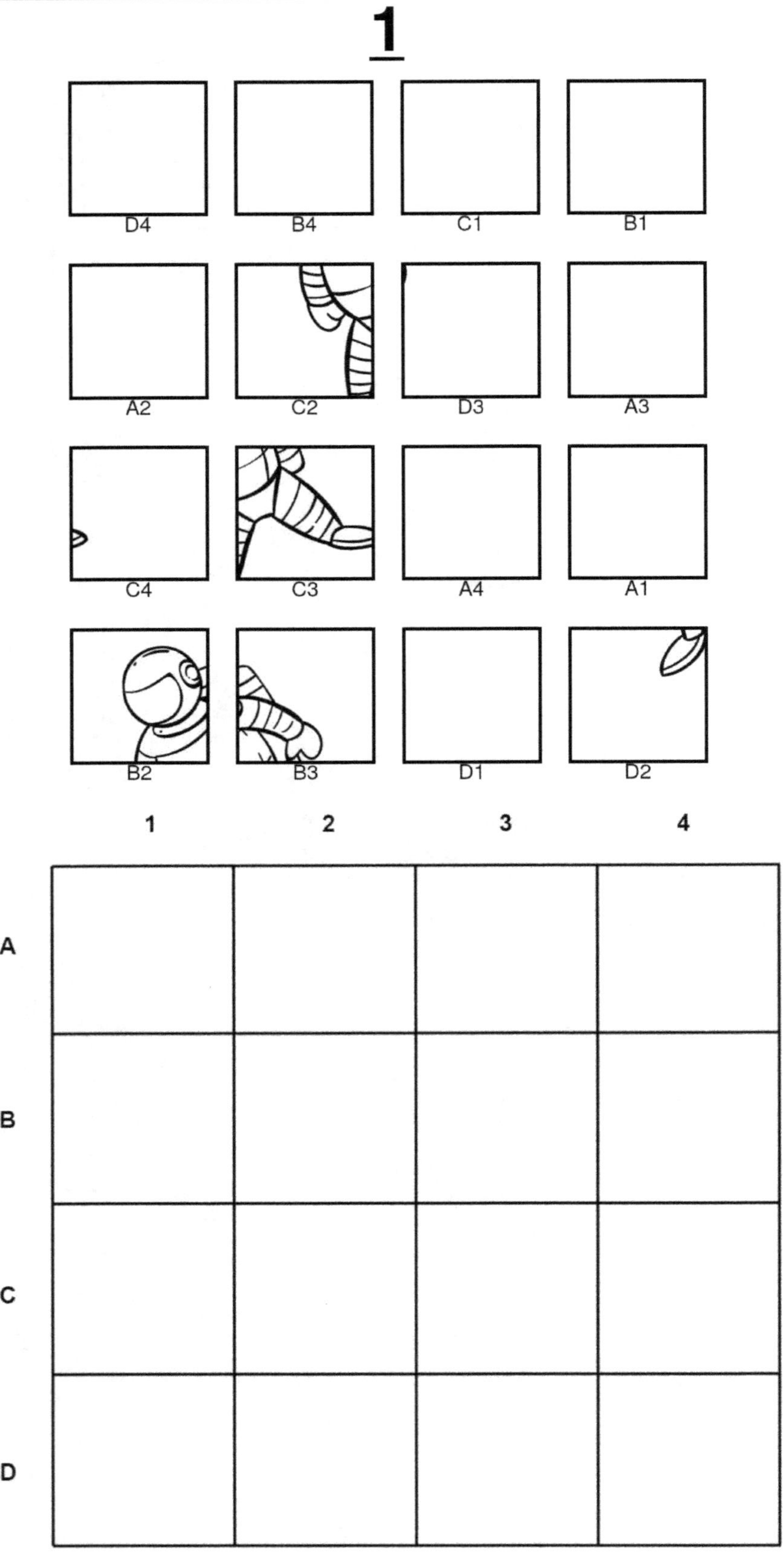

2

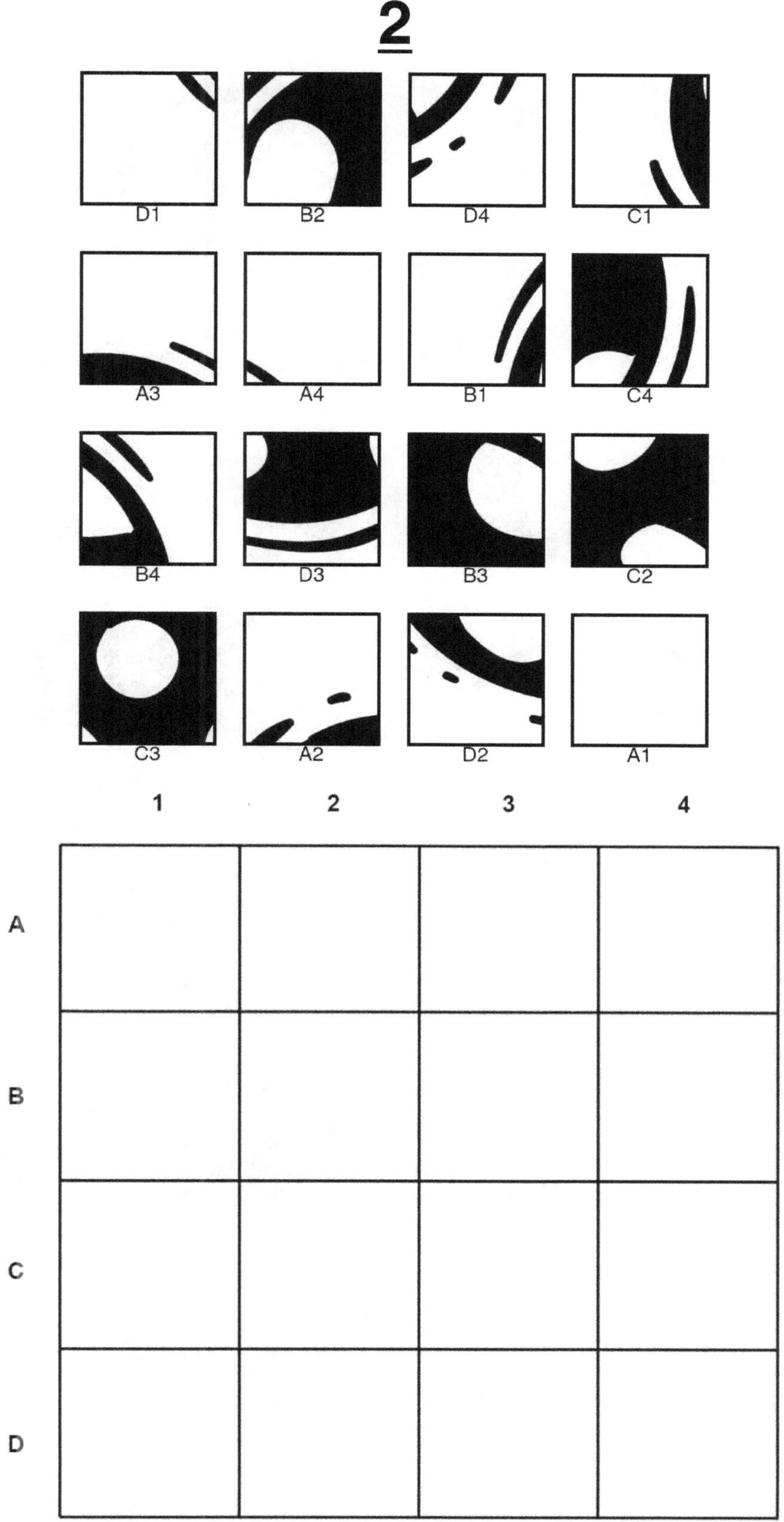

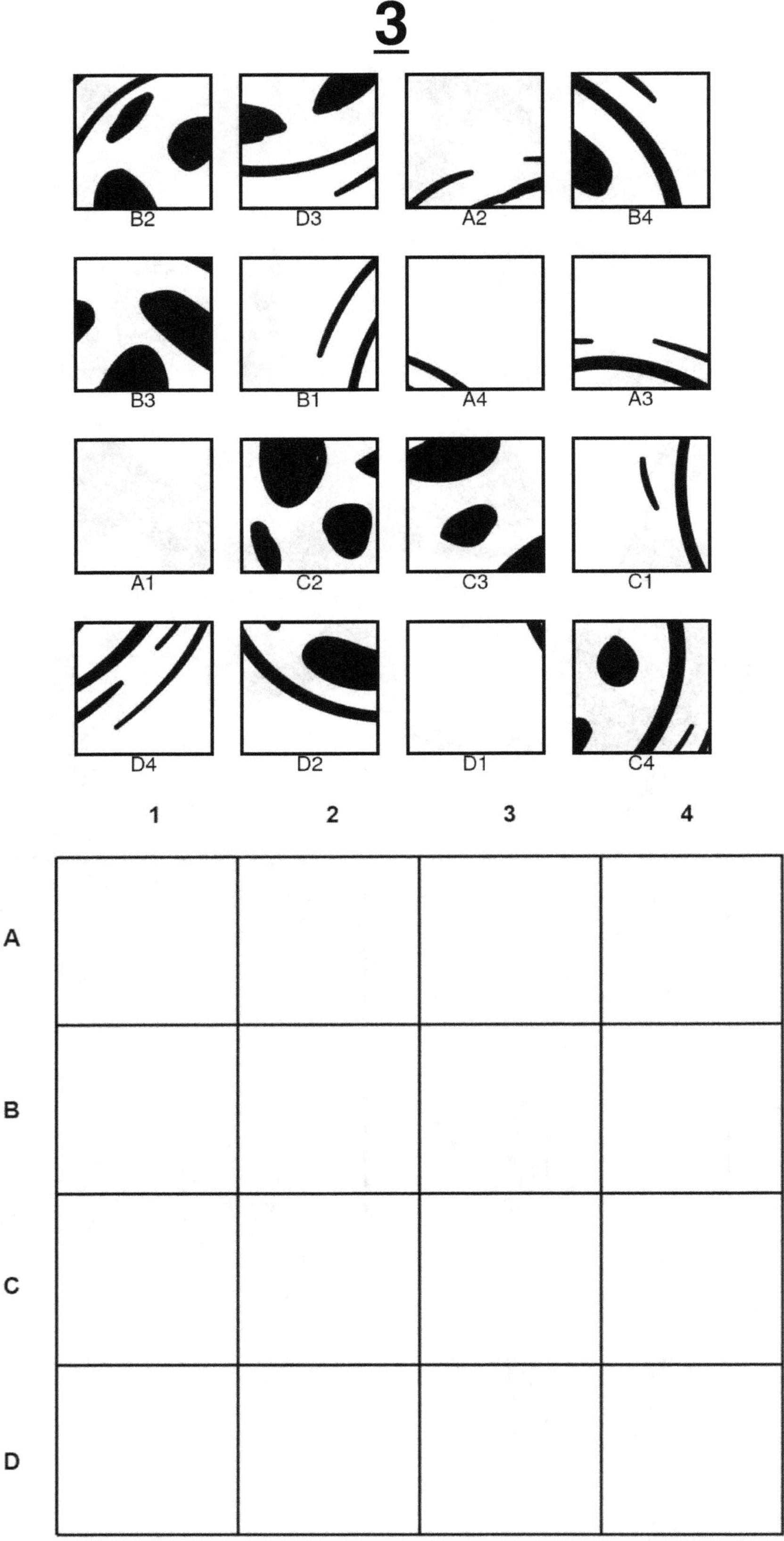
3
B2
D3
A2
B4
B3
B1
A4
A3
A1
C2
C3
C1
D4
D2
D1
C4
1
2
3
4
A
B
C
D

4

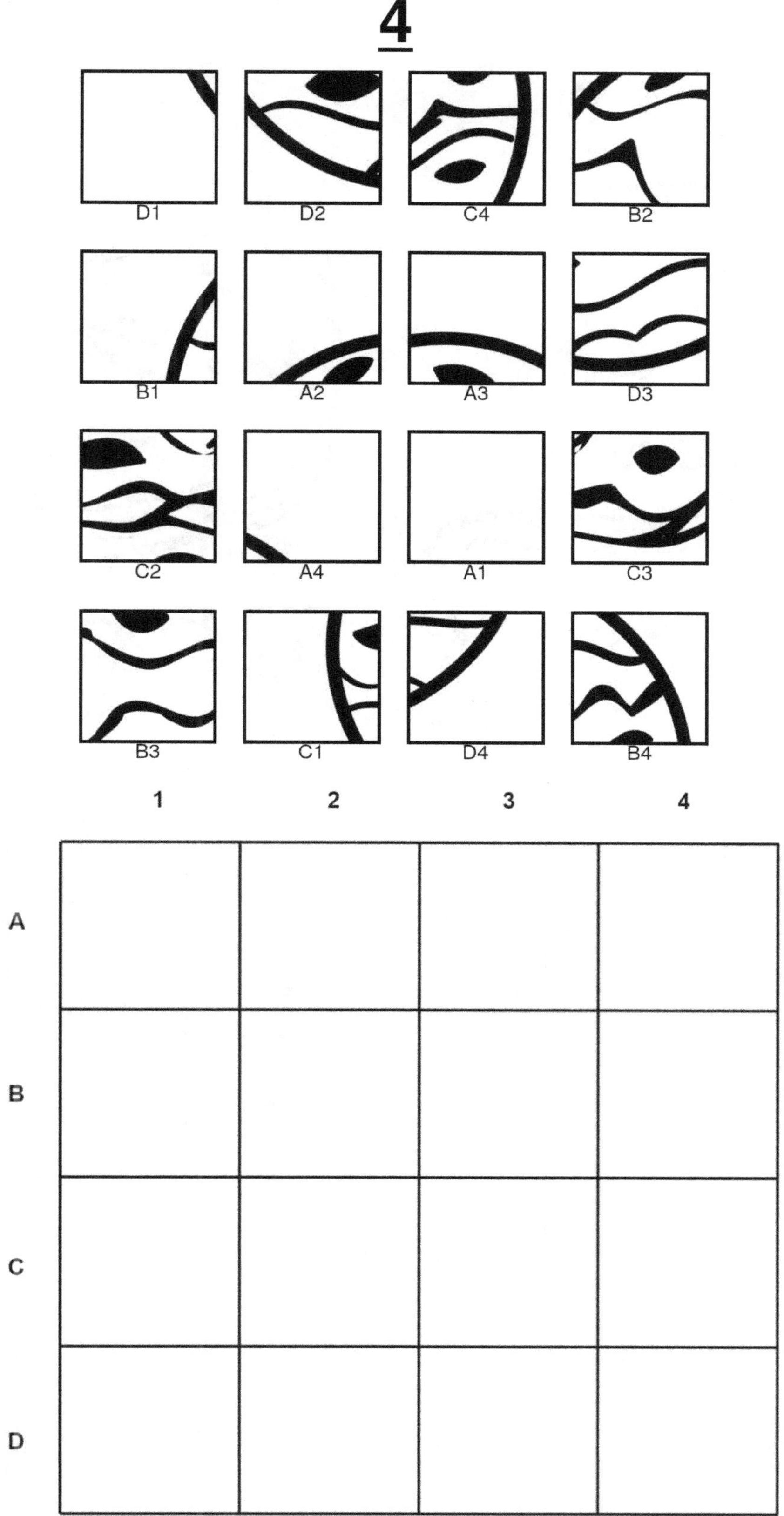

5

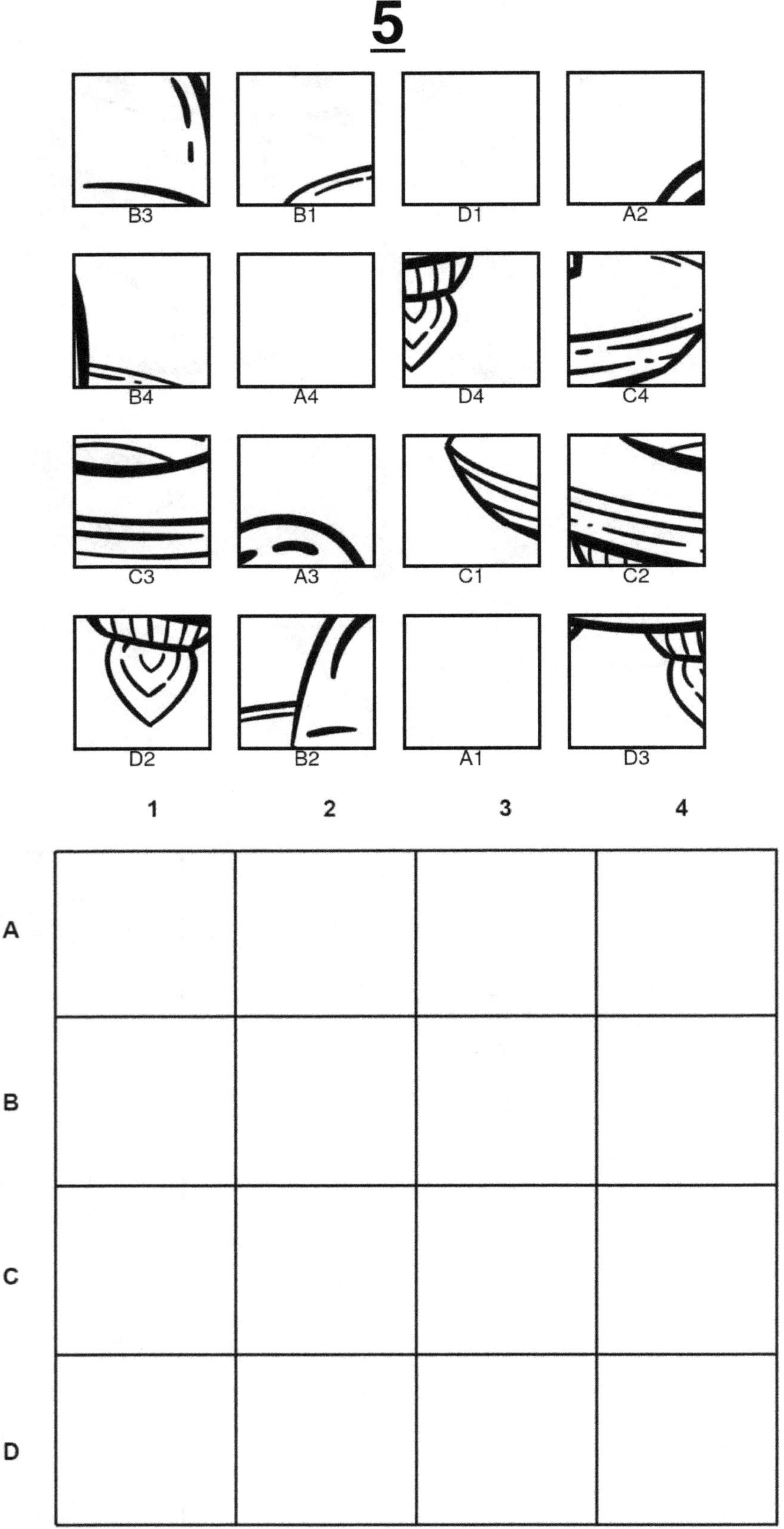

6

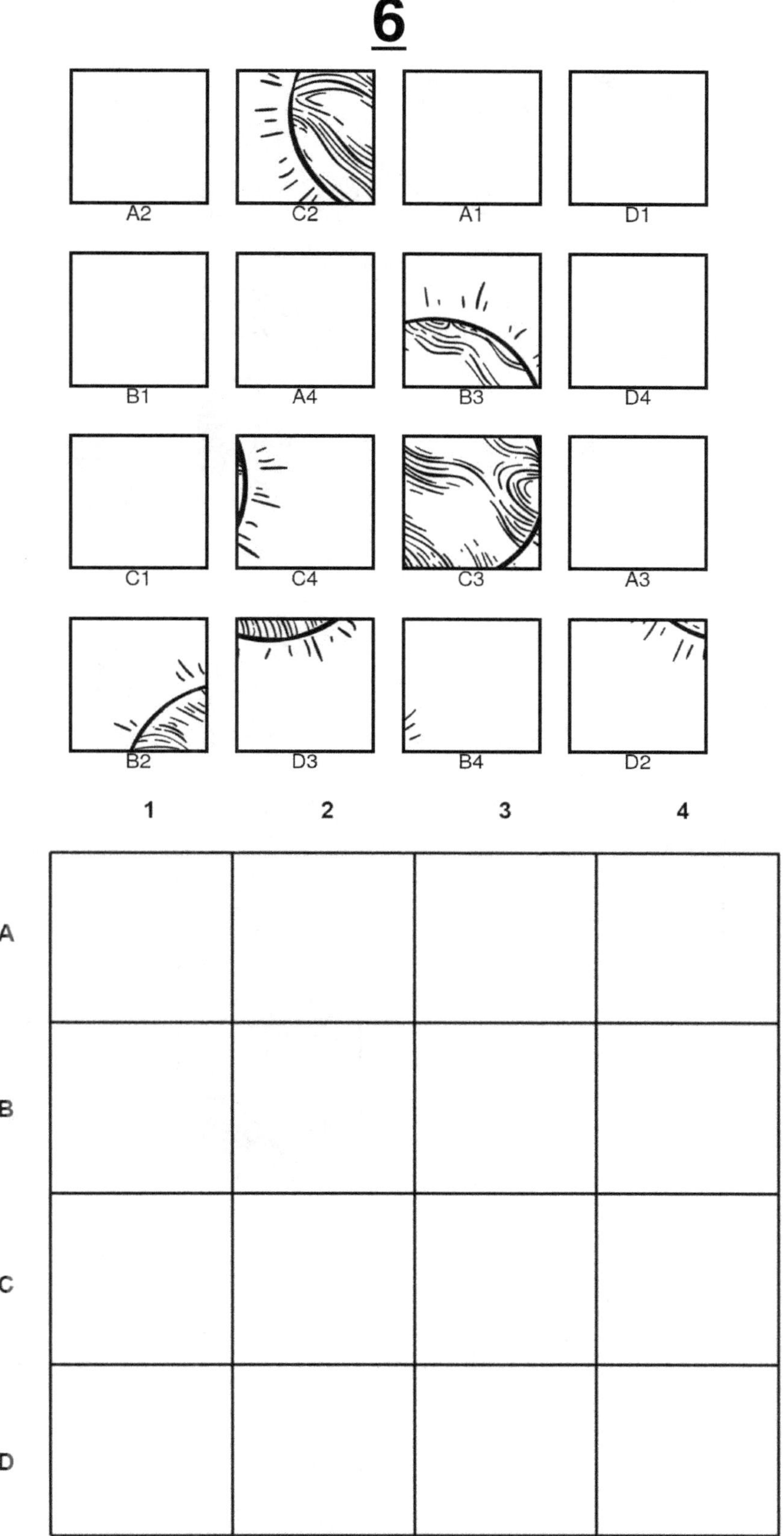

7

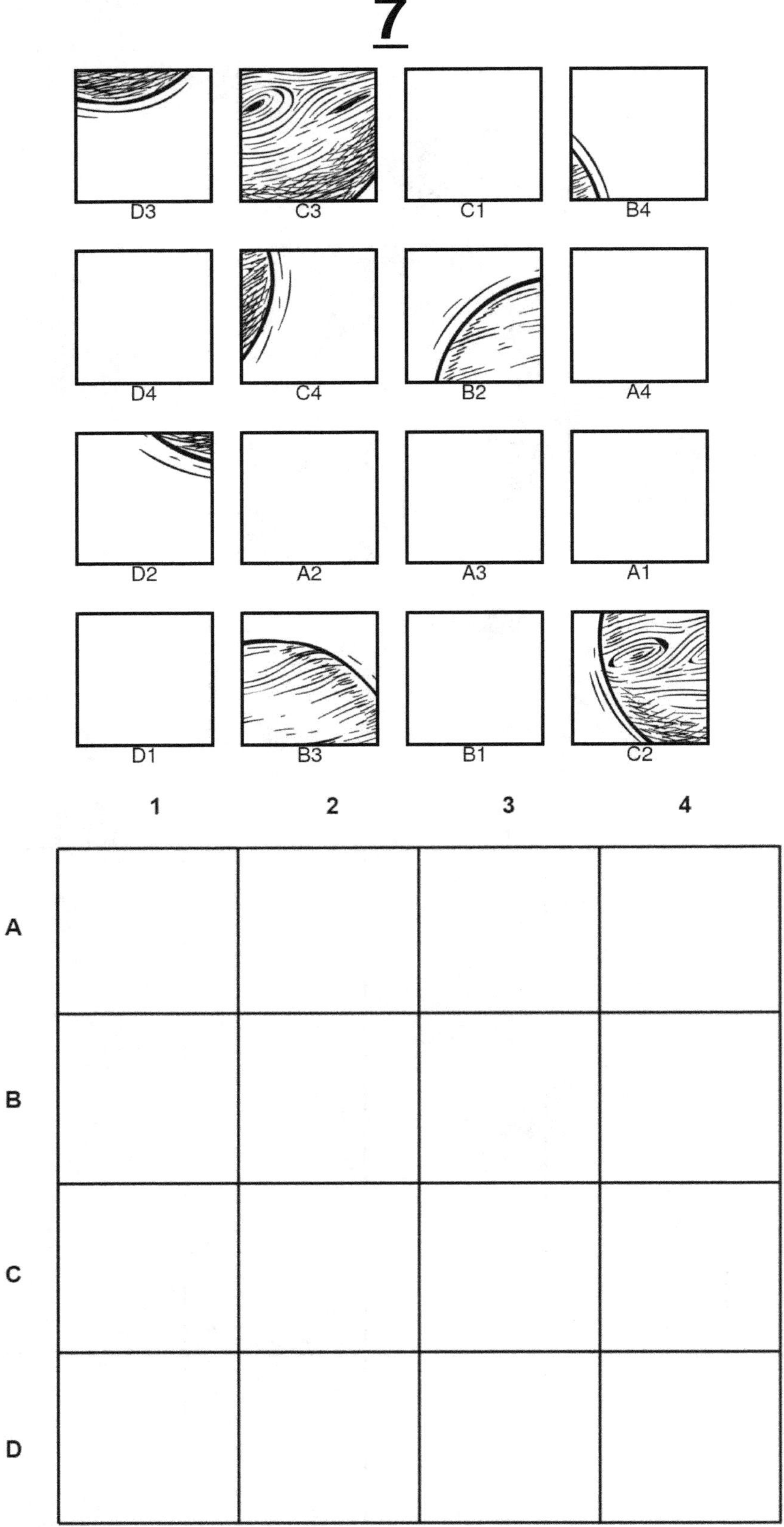

8

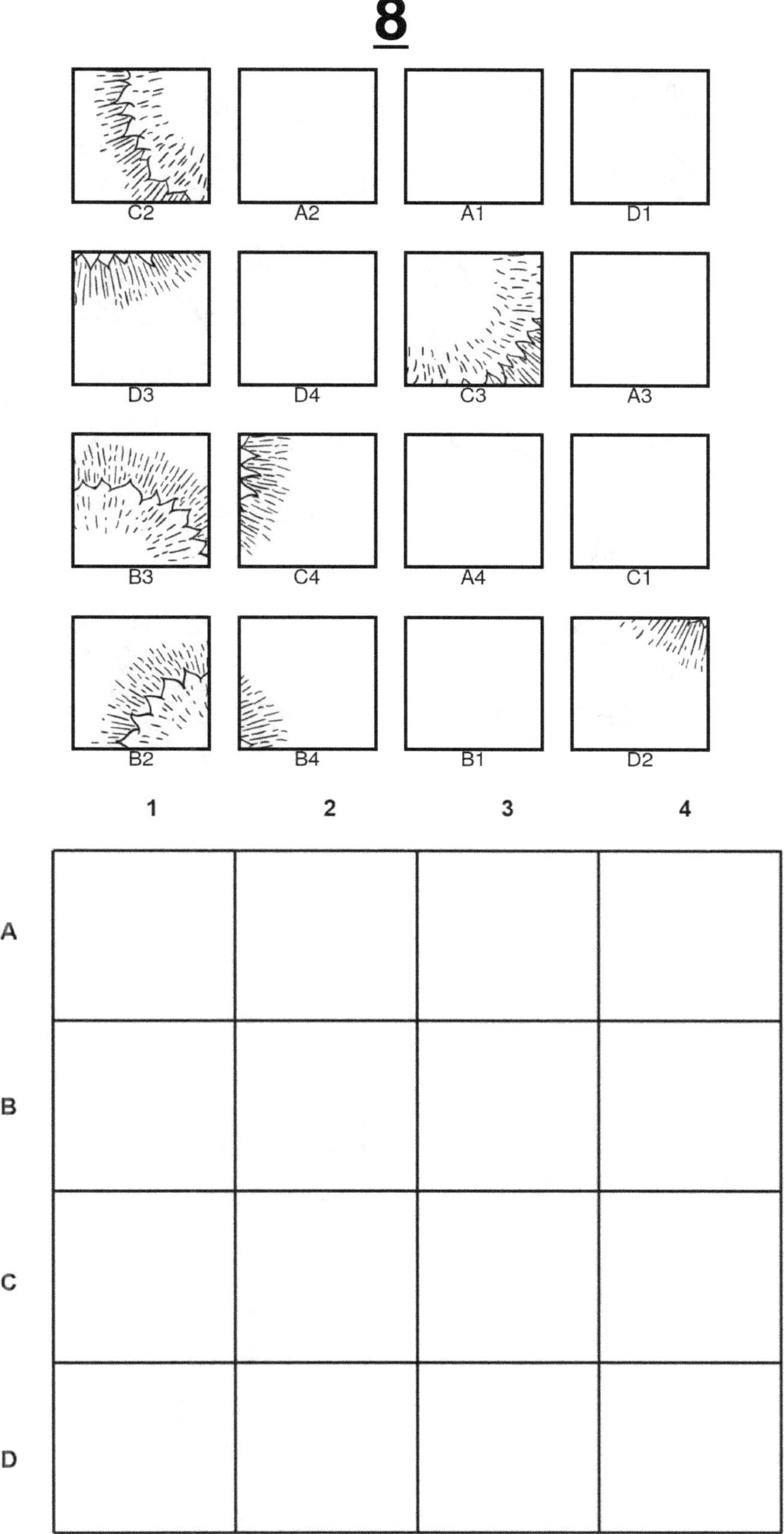

9
B3
B2
A4
C1
B1
C4
A1
C3
B4
D4
D2
D1
D3
A3
A2
C2
1
2
3
4
A
B
C
D

10

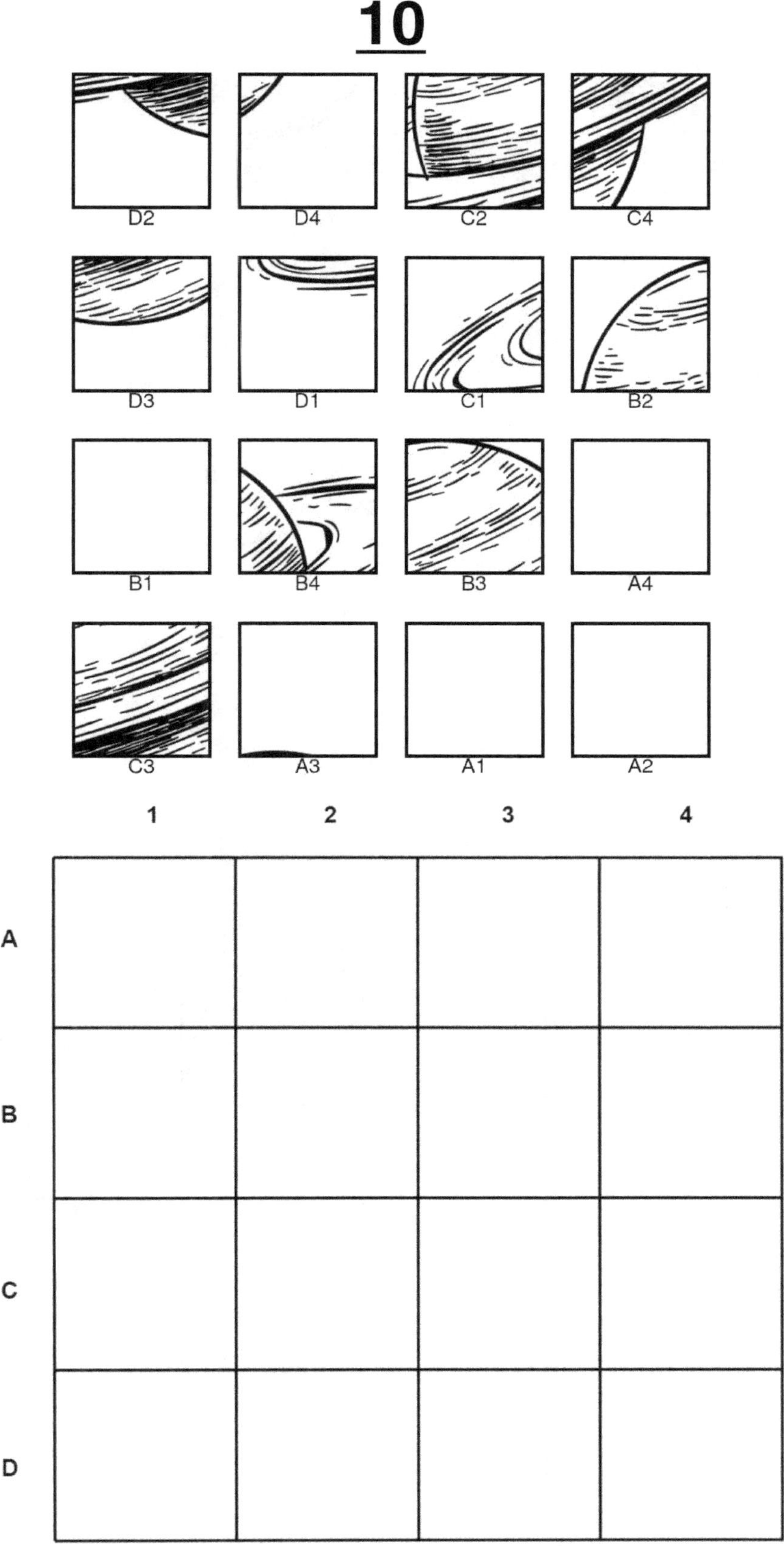

11

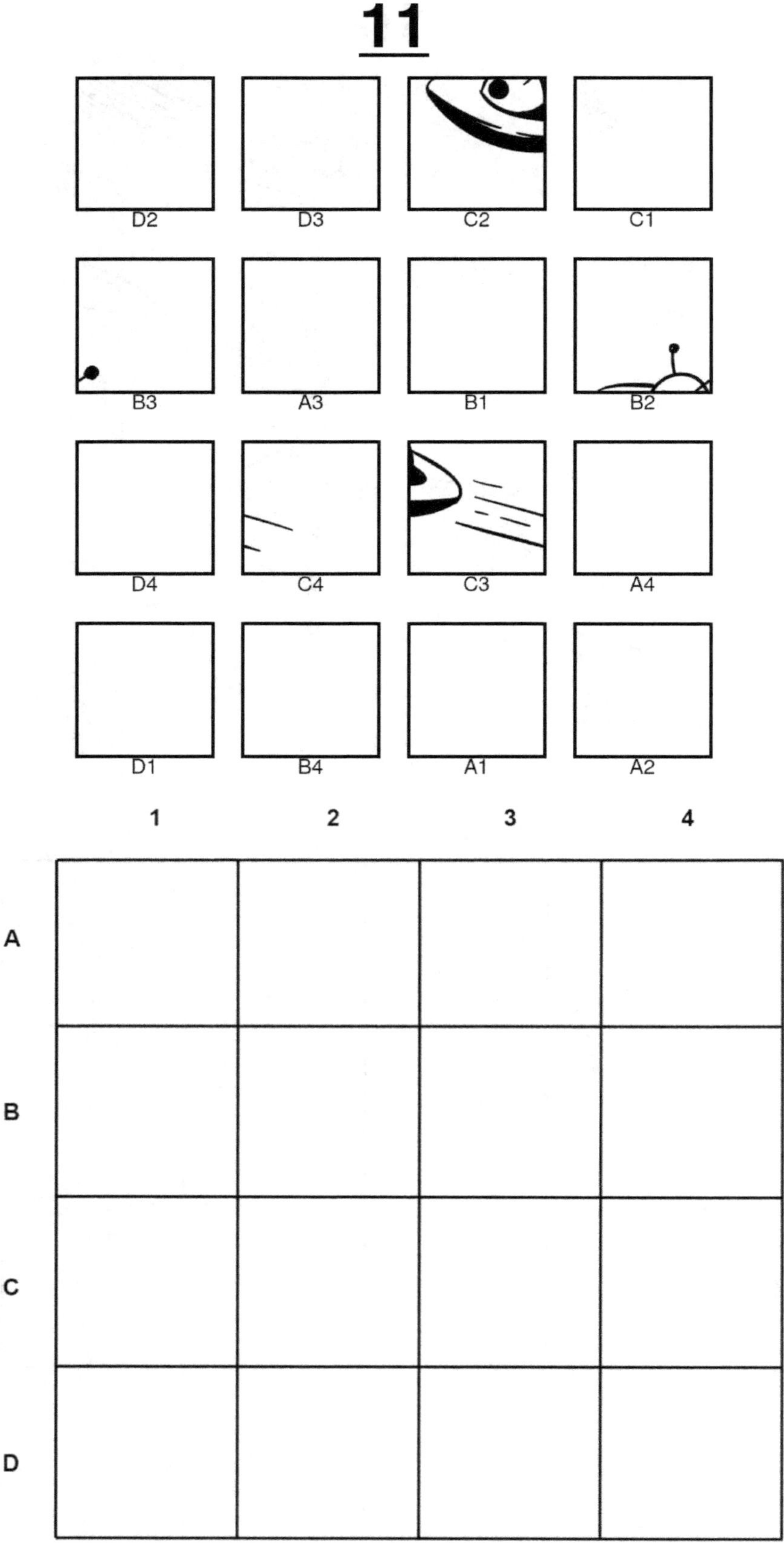

12

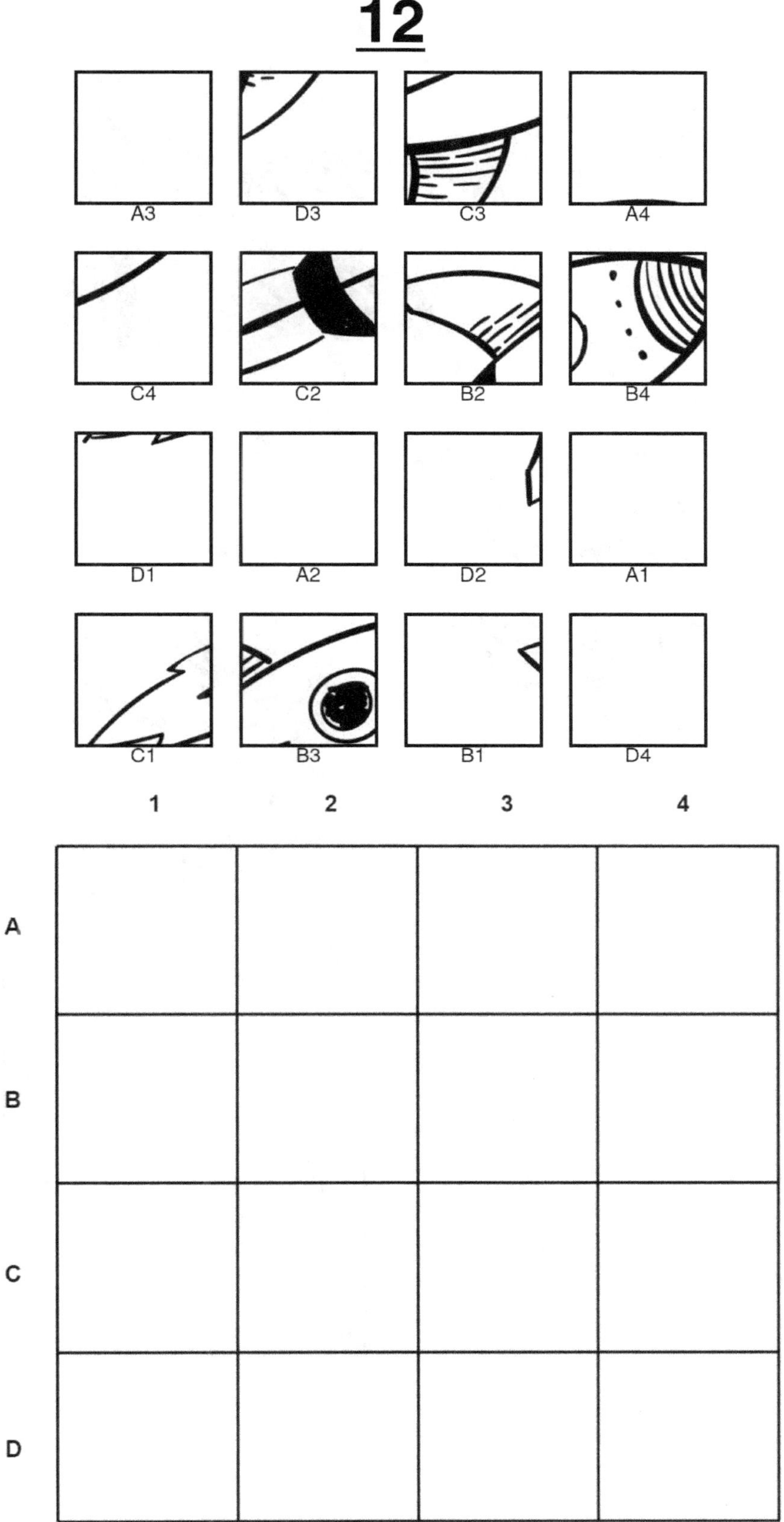

13

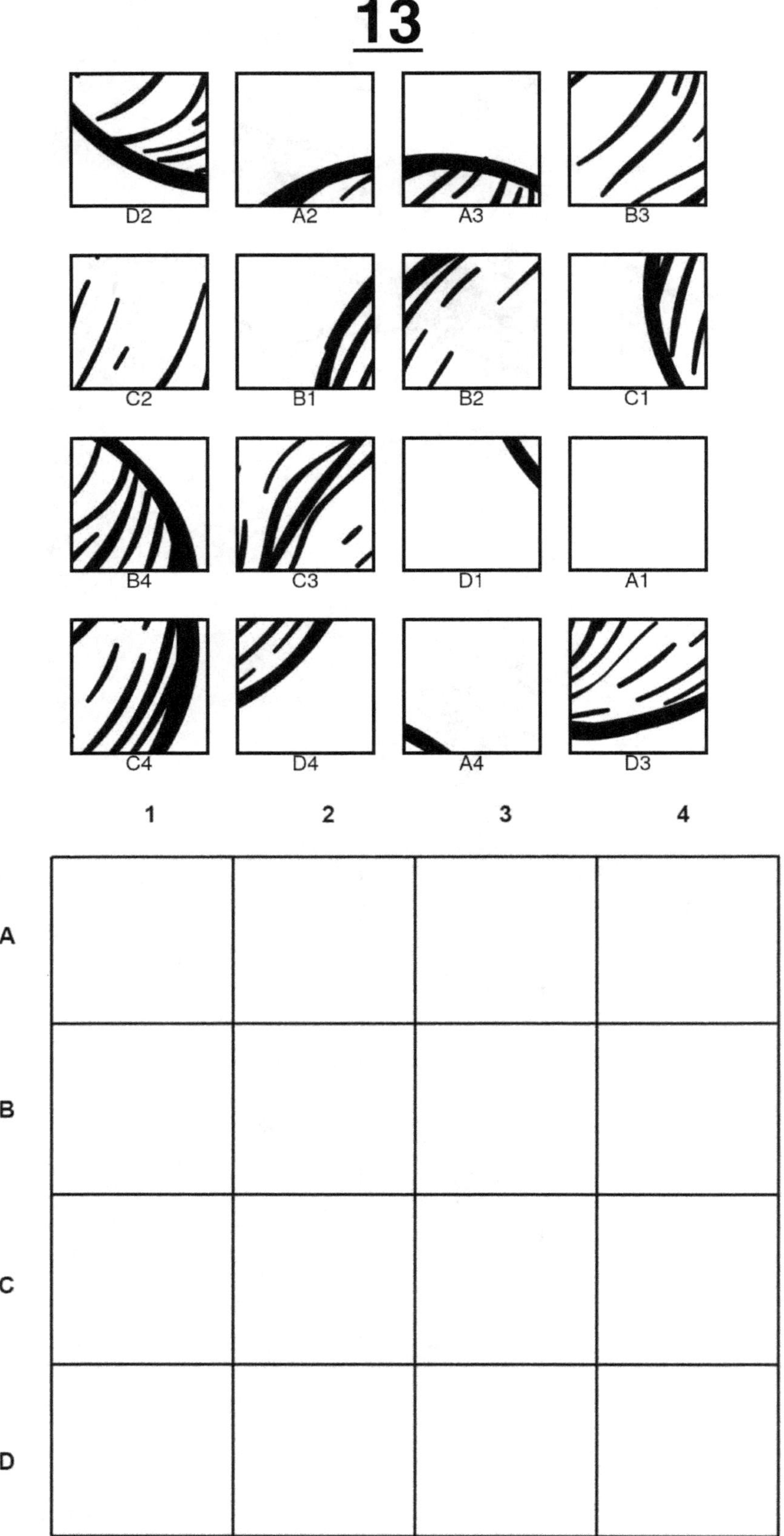

14

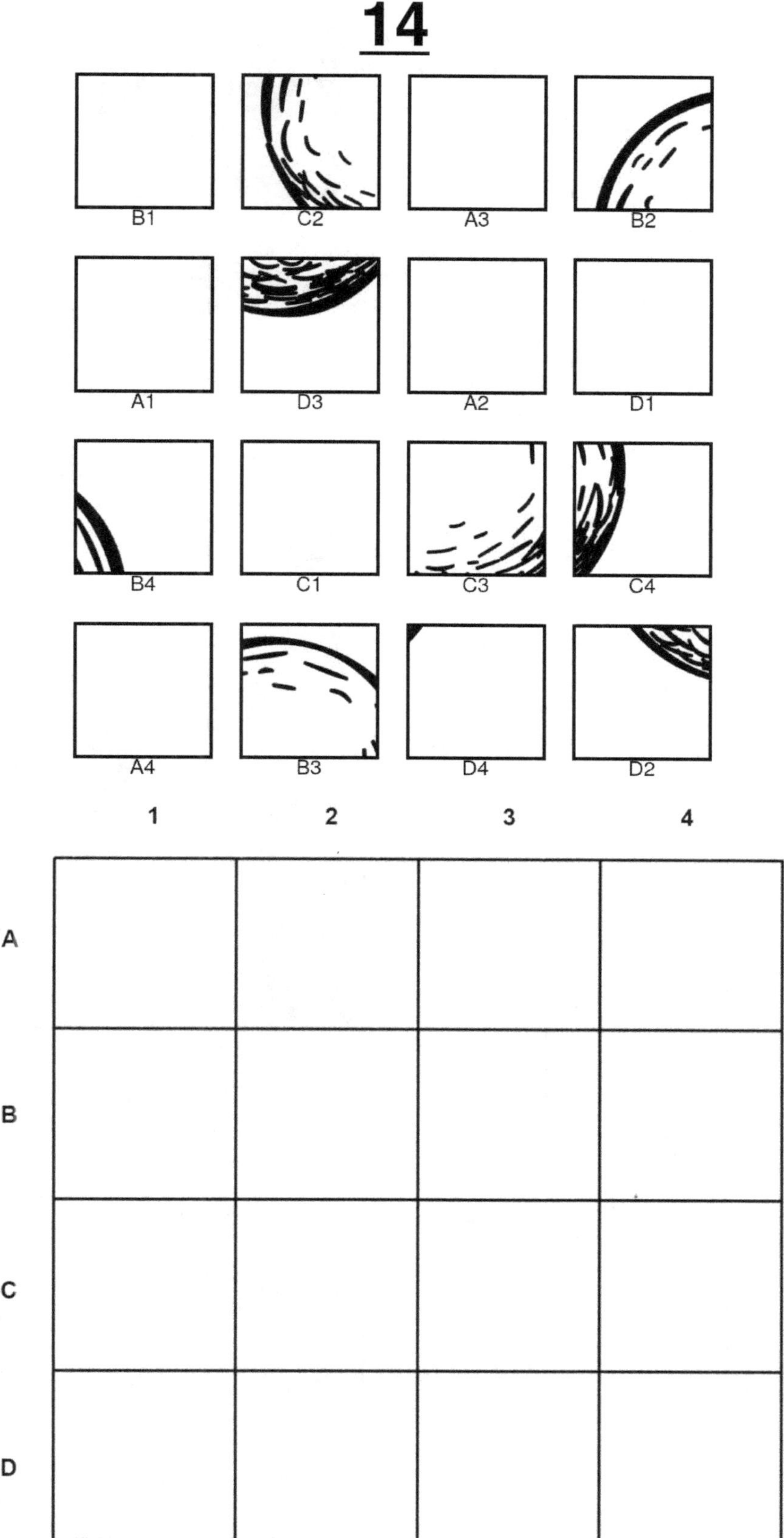

15

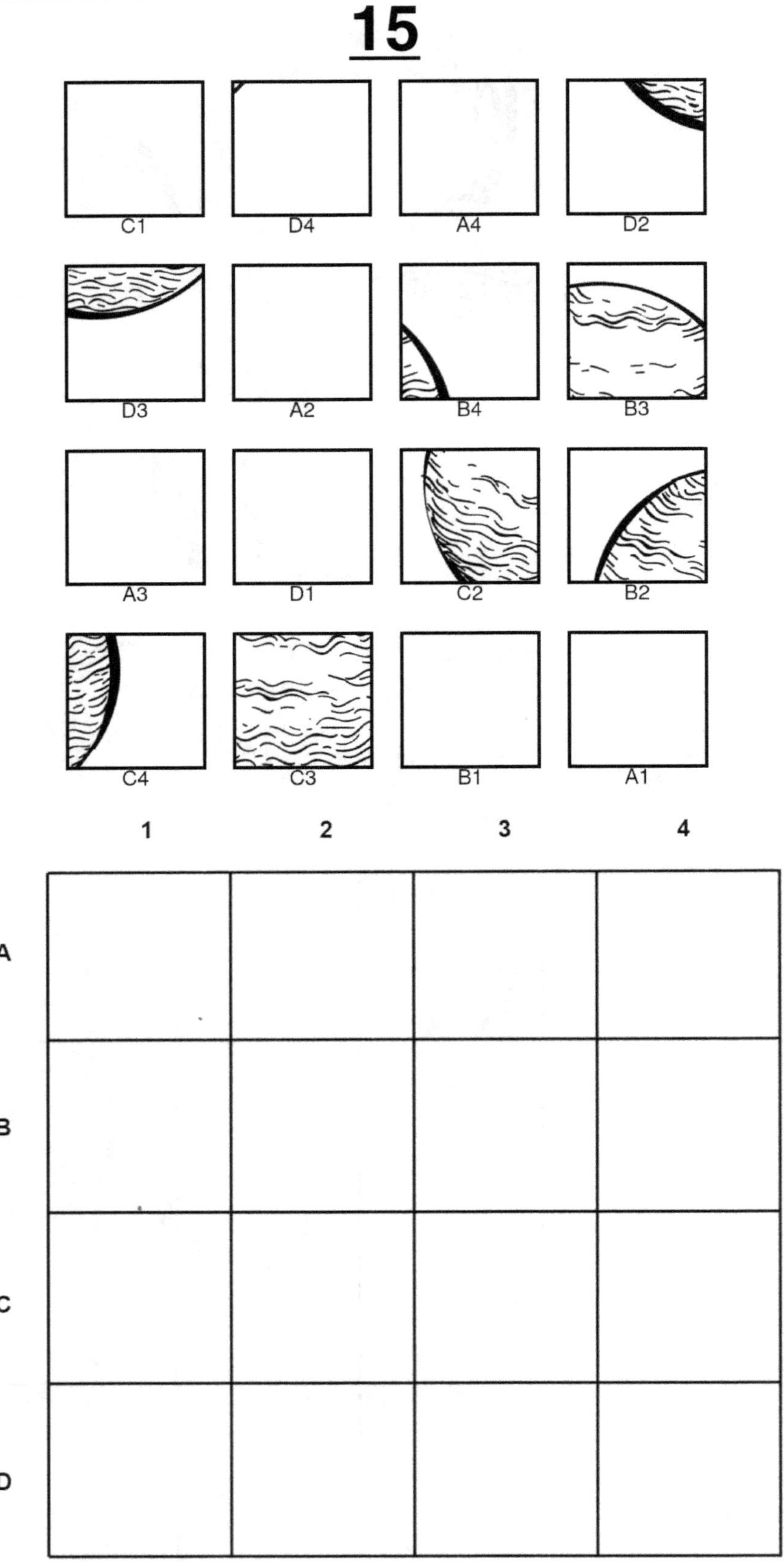

Word Search

Puzzle #1

COLUMBUS

```
N G N I L L I K H S A L M O N
A C F W E K R E S I L I E N T
V O M L D V C T S E N H F N U
I X U B U E I A A M P A F B I
G O W D T C C T T A B B U M V
A S B L Y W K L C D E I G P Q
T R Y T A O B Y A U R T W F Y
E I S R E G N A D R R A A O Q
E V P W E K A O H E A T H R Z
L E T A O V S L I A G T S G Z
C R U X L R O U L N M G I E J
I B Y V F H K C M E U A U O D
N A T I O N A L S K Y A S R N
M N J L A A I N C I D E N T H
N K H B E C N A R U D N E V P
```

BAHAMAS
DANGERS
DECLARATION
DESTRUCTIVE
DISCOVERY
DUTY
ENDURANCE
FORGE
GALLEY
HABITAT
HARDTACK
INCIDENT
KILLING
LUCKY
MUSKET
NATIONAL
NAVIGATE
NEST
RESILIENT
RIVERBANK
RUGGED
SALMON
UNION
WORK

Puzzle #11

THANKSGIVING

L	O	F	L	O	A	T	A	S	T	E	R	O	Z	H
W	A	C	B	L	Y	M	X	R	O	F	G	Q	Z	I
F	Y	L	R	A	E	L	O	C	A	L	L	A	M	S
H	O	E	O	N	A	C	B	R	E	A	K	Y	P	U
H	O	K	O	J	U	W	S	N	A	E	B	S	A	R
X	P	M	D	H	C	G	Q	B	G	G	E	T	S	T
R	N	E	E	R	G	J	Z	A	Y	R	G	Y	T	E
P	U	O	A	S	U	Q	L	Q	W	D	A	L	E	C
Y	N	O	D	C	V	O	M	A	O	T	N	V	H	I
K	V	E	Y	E	E	M	G	F	R	R	N	U	Y	E
P	W	X	T	T	V	Q	F	D	L	G	A	P	O	H
Q	E	Z	A	A	S	R	R	R	D	S	E	K	X	F
F	H	Y	T	N	L	E	E	P	I	G	T	R	D	Y
W	I	X	B	M	K	P	Z	S	T	E	E	B	V	R
U	C	Z	L	J	W	R	D	Y	G	Q	D	V	G	T

AROMA
BEANS
BEETS
BEGAN
BREAK
BROOD
CANOE
EARLY
FLOAT
FOUND
FRIED
GOURD
GRAVY
GREEN
HOMES
LARGE
LOCAL
PASTE
PEACE
PLATE
SERVE
SMALL
TASTE
WORLD
ZESTY

Puzzle #12

CHRISTMAS

E	H	C	H	B	S	U	R	P	R	I	S	E	S	D
A	V	F	F	T	R	A	L	L	E	R	B	M	U	L
T	H	E	M	E	Z	F	G	N	I	K	C	O	T	S
D	G	S	N	Q	T	F	A	M	O	U	S	Y	R	T
P	N	T	J	T	W	J	I	L	S	T	I	C	K	S
G	R	O	E	X	T	D	Y	U	L	E	T	I	D	E
L	E	O	Q	C	W	U	B	R	E	I	C	O	H	E
O	A	N	P	I	A	Z	Z	E	D	W	N	F	R	W
R	T	U	A	H	L	E	N	N	A	L	F	G	X	G
I	W	L	N	I	E	M	P	I	E	R	E	A	Q	U
O	L	J	Z	N	J	T	R	E	K	M	D	O	M	R
U	O	P	O	L	A	R	S	F	C	P	E	E	C	Z
S	H	O	C	K	H	B	D	W	C	N	M	S	D	Q
S	T	S	U	R	T	P	D	K	G	G	A	U	I	S
S	A	D	E	P	P	A	R	W	D	A	T	D	P	W

ANNUAL
BEARDED
DANCE
EVENT
FALLING
FAMOUS
FESTOON
FLANNEL
GLORIOUS
GROTTO
PEACE
POLAR
PROPHETS
PUMPKIN
SHOCK
SLED
STICKS
STOCKING
SURPRISES
THEME
TRUST
UMBRELLA
WISEMEN
WRAPPED

Puzzle #13

CHRISTMAS

C	E	L	E	B	R	A	T	E	L	R	Y	P	D	G
Q	T	S	F	A	T	I	N	K	L	I	N	G	G	E
S	Z	T	G	P	S	P	R	O	U	T	S	C	U	C
L	E	G	E	N	D	Y	F	U	N	O	W	B	C	H
E	T	V	P	A	I	L	R	A	P	U	Y	X	L	J
A	C	H	I	I	J	R	B	S	T	H	T	N	B	H
E	Y	W	G	T	C	Z	E	T	G	H	O	S	T	S
S	Q	R	S	I	A	T	S	H	T	U	E	Y	H	U
Y	E	X	O	T	R	L	U	D	T	A	H	R	O	C
D	K	V	T	G	F	B	E	R	O	A	T	A	L	X
R	J	C	L	R	E	I	O	R	E	X	G	Q	I	T
Z	M	P	I	E	T	T	G	N	I	X	O	B	D	Y
R	J	Z	G	T	M	C	A	N	E	S	Y	M	A	P
A	T	O	U	R	S	O	D	C	H	I	L	L	Y	W
F	U	K	E	M	Y	T	H	I	C	A	L	H	T	X

BONE
BOXING
BRIGHT
CANES
CATEGORY
CELEBRATE
CHILLY
EASY
ELVES
FATHER
GATHERINGS
GHOSTS
GIFTS
HOLIDAY
HOME
HUGS
LEGEND
MYTHICAL
NUTS
PICTURE
RELATIVES
SPROUTS
STICKY
TEA
TINKLING
TOURS

Puzzle #14

ANIMALS

D	H	A	D	G	S	H	E	E	P	L	F	W	C	G
W	H	H	I	W	E	E	V	I	L	D	A	H	J	M
H	J	N	A	E	C	A	T	S	U	R	C	L	F	W
Q	Y	L	T	S	L	U	N	A	M	O	T	H	H	X
C	C	Q	O	F	L	O	W	A	R	D	N	U	T	Q
R	I	L	M	T	C	B	X	C	E	I	W	F	N	V
I	G	O	Y	E	Z	U	D	O	R	Y	G	W	C	A
V	Z	G	K	B	F	F	P	C	L	S	O	R	D	V
E	Y	I	A	V	C	F	T	K	Y	V	F	R	J	L
R	E	X	N	Y	L	A	F	R	H	C	D	C	G	X
O	E	C	G	U	L	L	N	O	E	R	N	J	V	Z
T	R	Q	A	Z	W	O	T	A	R	S	I	E	R	F
T	K	Z	R	B	K	S	O	C	R	H	U	S	K	Y
E	O	W	O	C	A	E	S	H	E	Y	X	F	J	S
R	H	L	O	B	S	T	E	R	U	Y	T	S	U	A

BUFFALO
CANARY
COCKROACH
CRUSTACEAN
DIATOM
DORY
GULL
HUSKY
KANGAROO
LOBSTER
LUNA MOTH
LYNX
RIVER OTTER
SEA COW
SHEEP
TARSIER
TUNA
TUNDRA WOLF
WEEVIL

Puzzle #15

COLUMBUS

U	N	O	I	T	A	L	O	S	I	C	L	H	S	R
N	S	X	U	M	Y	R	A	T	I	N	A	S	H	E
I	E	E	E	F	M	I	C	S	N	D	R	Z	K	C
V	F	O	M	D	G	U	B	K	V	C	T	C	I	O
E	C	I	T	I	Z	E	N	S	H	I	P	G	V	V
R	S	H	O	G	D	M	L	E	V	A	R	T	P	E
S	Y	N	R	N	G	E	Y	A	N	T	H	E	M	R
A	T	W	V	I	O	R	F	D	Z	N	N	T	J	Y
L	U	F	D	T	S	O	Z	E	R	O	O	A	K	N
M	R	G	I	Y	H	T	C	A	N	A	R	Y	R	T
D	E	S	E	R	T	I	O	N	E	C	H	E	J	G
Y	W	O	U	N	D	S	S	P	I	C	E	S	S	G
L	L	A	F	D	N	A	L	E	H	H	P	S	G	R
E	G	A	Y	O	V	Y	G	A	R	E	D	A	E	L
T	F	Y	C	A	D	B	H	C	A	R	R	A	C	K

ANTHEM
AZORES
CANARY
CARRACK
CHRISTOPHER
CITIZENSHIP
DEFENCES
DESERTION
DIGNITY
DRIFTS
GRANT
HARDY
IMMUNE
ISOLATION
LANDFALL
LEADER
RECOVERY
ROT
SANITARY
SPICES
TRAVEL
UNIVERSAL
VOYAGE
WOUNDS

Puzzle #16

THANKSGIVING

A	R	A	J	O	P	D	E	T	I	N	U	M	L	I
G	E	U	Q	I	N	U	S	T	S	X	W	Y	Z	K
A	A	W	O	E	L	B	G	W	R	T	D	O	A	K
L	L	D	B	V	L	E	N	R	F	U	S	N	M	G
O	E	D	A	R	A	P	V	O	O	E	G	I	J	P
T	N	G	K	N	E	S	G	A	S	U	E	O	R	B
S	H	W	I	I	A	Y	M	E	R	A	P	N	Y	K
K	S	R	N	V	S	C	A	J	M	T	E	S	W	A
I	F	E	G	M	I	S	R	R	N	T	H	S	N	T
X	R	K	R	F	U	N	E	H	P	C	U	U	R	M
H	E	E	N	T	O	T	G	S	T	E	N	N	C	K
B	N	D	H	L	S	U	U	X	F	L	G	R	B	X
U	C	B	T	T	O	R	R	A	C	E	R	R	O	V
C	H	E	L	P	A	T	S	T	R	R	Y	T	F	R
W	I	N	T	E	R	F	Y	X	H	Y	L	Z	S	J

AUTUMN
BAKING
CANADA
CARROT
CELERY
FATHER
FOURTH
FRENCH
GIVING
GROUPS
HUNGRY
KISSES
NUTMEG
ONIONS
PARADE
PRAYER
SAVOUR
SEASON
STAPLE
STRESS
TRAVEL
UNIQUE
UNITED
WINTER
YOGURT

Puzzle #2

GARDENING

V	E	E	F	R	S	O	R	C	X	X	S	S	Y	T
F	E	N	R	U	R	L	U	T	U	S	H	E	A	R
X	J	P	S	U	M	A	A	O	G	L	T	W	K	U
H	W	M	O	B	T	I	R	T	J	P	T	T	H	N
O	H	T	C	R	N	L	G	E	E	X	R	U	A	K
R	Q	O	N	H	T	O	U	A	T	P	O	C	R	W
T	U	R	Q	E	O	O	I	C	T	M	C	D	M	E
I	A	I	N	G	M	I	I	T	I	I	K	M	O	T
C	N	G	S	U	G	N	C	L	C	R	O	J	N	L
U	T	I	X	G	R	X	O	E	E	E	G	N	I	A
L	I	N	H	M	O	S	E	R	N	H	L	A	O	N
T	T	A	X	T	W	S	E	P	I	X	T	E	U	D
U	Y	L	Q	N	E	P	O	R	F	V	W	O	S	S
R	E	N	E	D	R	A	G	V	Y	B	N	L	L	N
E	L	P	H	A	N	G	I	N	G	F	L	E	E	C

AGRICULTURE
CHOICE
CLOTH
CULTURE
ENVIRONMENT
FUMIGATION
GARDENER
GROWER
HANGING
HARMONIOUS
HELIOTROPE
HORTICULTURE
NURSERY
OPEN
ORIGINAL
PETALS
QUANTITY
RARE
ROCK
SELECTION
SHEAR
TRUNK
WETLANDS

Puzzle #3

THANKSGIVING

B	I	X	R	A	B	B	I	T	S	E	E	C	O	K
A	T	S	J	E	D	B	X	S	S	P	I	C	E	S
Q	L	V	A	R	I	E	T	Y	E	E	R	T	T	R
Q	K	C	M	Z	S	F	A	K	E	P	V	O	C	Q
N	A	P	K	I	N	E	L	R	R	G	I	R	U	X
O	F	I	T	D	N	I	A	A	R	O	A	C	A	T
S	A	C	R	E	D	U	G	F	V	I	W	Y	E	H
W	J	T	E	H	A	F	T	I	O	O	V	T	O	R
O	C	U	F	E	Y	L	V	E	R	O	U	E	E	V
R	J	R	R	W	F	G	L	S	W	O	D	R	D	N
S	W	E	H	E	L	F	S	E	L	P	P	A	A	U
H	O	O	E	M	P	V	O	F	R	A	N	C	E	H
I	L	R	B	E	J	P	M	C	L	G	Q	W	E	T
P	G	N	J	E	H	Q	E	L	U	F	Y	O	J	O
V	I	S	I	O	N	I	S	P	I	N	R	U	T	W

ALLERGY
APPLES
ARRIVED
COFFEE
FLAVOUR
FRANCE
HARVEST
JOYFUL
MINUTE
NAPKIN
NETWORK
ORIGIN
PEPPER
PICTURE
RABBIT
RECIPES
SACRED
SEAFOOD
SPICES
SPROUT
TURNIPS
VARIETY
VISION
VOYAGE
WORSHIP

Puzzle #4

FRUITS

K	S	U	O	I	C	I	L	E	D	U	T	C	K	G
W	C	I	J	V	T	E	R	O	O	M	C	Z	Q	R
N	A	A	V	J	L	E	P	A	R	G	A	E	S	A
Y	O	Y	I	E	N	I	R	A	D	N	A	M	C	N
F	R	L	O	M	E	S	L	G	R	A	N	A	D	A
P	Y	R	E	M	I	C	A	C	O	G	U	M	F	D
L	O	C	E	M	I	T	B	I	L	I	M	B	I	I
A	P	L	E	B	Y	R	O	T	U	I	R	A	Y	L
N	U	Q	E	M	D	R	E	L	L	A	Q	R	A	L
T	L	B	T	M	P	U	A	H	L	V	B	E	N	A
A	A	W	M	S	O	E	O	N	C	O	Z	L	G	V
I	S	A	B	I	A	P	D	L	A	L	P	L	M	V
N	A	Z	E	M	E	T	Z	A	C	C	P	A	E	R
S	N	N	B	N	O	L	E	M	K	S	U	M	I	O
E	M	I	R	A	C	L	E	F	R	U	I	T	C	U

AMBARELLA
APOLLO
BILIMBI
CAIMITO
CANARYMELON
CEMPEDAK
CHERIMOYA
CLOUDBERRY
DELICIOUS
GRANADA
GRANADILLA
GRAPE
ICACO
MANDARINE
MIRACLEFRUIT
MOORE
MUSKMELON
NAZEMETZ
PLANTAINS
POMELO
PULASAN
SEAGRAPE
YANGMEI

Puzzle #5

HALLOWEEN

H	S	S	L	L	A	B	E	Y	E	W	W	O	Q	J
W	N	J	G	I	P	L	G	L	L	M	M	L	C	Z
H	S	I	L	I	V	E	D	B	U	T	P	C	O	V
V	X	Q	Q	U	M	E	Y	G	H	O	S	T	L	Y
F	F	M	K	O	F	Y	V	E	S	M	H	A	C	T
R	L	L	A	F	E	D	X	C	P	G	E	G	H	X
I	A	J	Y	F	L	R	A	G	U	A	K	F	H	G
G	S	I	B	R	F	E	W	E	Q	I	T	A	A	Q
H	H	M	D	I	R	S	D	N	R	Z	F	C	R	G
T	L	G	F	G	I	S	K	I	V	D	F	E	H	G
E	I	N	O	H	G	U	I	E	A	V	M	P	A	O
N	G	O	F	T	H	P	W	F	Y	R	I	A	F	R
I	H	K	R	E	T	H	G	I	F	E	R	I	F	Y
N	T	Z	A	N	Y	N	Y	B	F	S	G	N	A	F
G	Q	I	H	S	I	L	U	O	H	G	E	T	U	G

DEVILISH
DREADFUL
DRESSUP
ELF
EVIL
EYEBALLS
EYEPATCH
FACE PAINT
FAIRY
FALL
FANGS
FEAR
FIREFIGHTER
FLASHLIGHT
FOG
FRIGHT
FRIGHTEN
FRIGHTENING
GENIE
GHASTLY
GHOST
GHOSTLY
GHOUL
GHOULISH
GORY

Puzzle #6

GARDENING

M	V	W	P	N	H	A	R	E	S	O	U	R	C	E
Y	H	I	Z	A	Q	Y	T	Z	F	X	C	Z	R	P
Z	S	T	O	A	B	Q	B	K	M	Y	U	F	E	L
E	H	H	Y	K	R	O	O	R	A	V	T	R	S	A
C	R	E	L	H	E	R	T	O	I	F	T	A	I	N
S	U	R	G	I	R	J	A	A	L	D	I	G	S	T
I	B	L	I	O	S	L	N	N	N	N	N	R	T	I
M	R	A	T	K	L	G	I	Q	G	I	G	A	A	N
P	I	E	N	I	V	U	C	R	T	E	S	N	N	G
L	O	I	F	U	V	B	A	V	E	M	M	T	C	S
I	H	K	X	N	I	A	L	X	I	D	Z	E	E	R
C	U	L	T	I	V	A	T	I	O	N	R	V	N	X
I	Y	R	A	T	N	E	M	E	L	P	M	O	C	T
T	B	T	T	G	N	I	G	G	I	D	V	Y	B	R
Y	A	Y	D	A	I	M	P	A	T	I	E	N	T	S

ARRANGEMENT
BORDER
BOTANICAL
BOTANIST
COMPLEMENTARY
CULTIVATE
CULTIVATION
CUTTINGS

DIGGING
FRAGRANT
HYBRID
IMPATIENTS
PLANTINGS
RESISTANCE
RESOURCE
RHYTHM

SHRUB
SIMPLICITY
SOIL
VINE
WITHER

Puzzle #7

VALENTINES

P	D	O	I	T	G	N	I	N	E	T	S	I	L	Y
A	E	T	A	M	H	C	U	P	C	A	K	E	G	S
Z	I	V	T	B	M	G	T	B	L	I	E	V	W	T
O	R	D	T	Q	U	T	I	J	E	R	H	C	M	U
J	E	W	E	L	S	D	K	L	V	Y	H	O	E	X
B	L	E	N	S	J	Q	G	K	E	H	P	M	Y	E
L	A	A	D	I	P	U	C	E	R	L	X	P	W	D
S	T	A	A	F	F	I	N	I	T	Y	D	A	A	O
E	I	D	N	A	L	R	A	G	C	I	I	N	B	H
R	V	R	C	Q	W	G	D	U	A	I	N	I	A	T
E	E	S	E	I	L	I	O	D	D	O	N	O	R	C
N	S	A	R	R	O	W	W	R	C	E	E	N	R	T
I	O	F	F	I	C	I	A	L	S	I	R	A	P	L
T	W	P	F	O	R	E	T	T	E	L	E	V	O	L
Y	S	Y	S	A	R	C	N	Y	S	O	I	D	I	S

AFFINITY
ARROW
ATTENDANCE
BUDGET
CANDLELIGHT
CLEVER
COMPANION
CUPCAKE
CUPID
DINNER
DOILIES
GARLAND
HAPPY
IDIOSYNCRASY
JEWELS
LISTENING
LOVE LETTER
MATE
OFFICIAL
PARIS
RED
RELATIVES
SERENITY
TUXEDO

Puzzle #8

THANKSGIVING

R	F	S	M	T	X	O	R	G	E	A	O	D	T	R
Q	S	Q	Y	M	E	E	Z	E	E	R	F	V	K	E
F	F	K	E	M	T	H	Y	R	H	L	A	H	Z	L
D	Z	G	N	Y	B	Q	E	M	H	T	B	F	E	I
X	Q	P	N	A	T	O	S	A	B	I	A	B	P	S
I	S	C	I	I	H	N	L	N	R	T	V	G	O	H
H	L	I	R	E	T	T	U	B	K	T	S	U	P	G
B	C	E	S	O	F	A	V	O	U	R	H	H	B	T
S	E	R	A	T	W	S	E	R	B	J	B	X	L	U
O	T	O	A	D	E	D	E	S	S	F	S	H	D	R
Y	T	S	L	E	E	R	S	V	T	T	M	V	M	K
P	T	A	E	I	S	R	F	V	A	A	E	P	J	E
T	Z	E	T	I	V	N	I	Y	T	E	E	E	Y	Y
I	Q	D	O	O	R	E	I	U	U	L	L	R	W	R
S	I	I	H	A	P	P	S	Y	T	A	E	R	T	S

BOUNTY
BUTTER
CROWDS
EATING
FAVOUR
FREEZE
GATHER
GERMAN
GOBBLE
HEARTH
INVITE
LEADER
LEAVES
OLIVES
POTATO
PRIEST
RELISH
SEARCH
SISTER
SWEETS
SYMBOL
THANKS
TREATS
TREATY
TURKEY

Puzzle #9

ANIMALS

E	O	Q	Q	N	I	L	O	G	N	A	P	F	P	Z
G	B	V	X	A	C	L	L	L	I	R	D	N	A	M
V	W	A	M	O	H	W	R	F	J	C	S	T	P	O
K	N	R	S	B	I	N	B	J	F	T	E	R	G	E
E	Y	O	I	K	M	Y	O	D	E	I	K	W	N	A
K	N	U	M	P	I	H	C	I	O	C	T	S	N	U
M	V	F	F	L	P	N	C	N	L	T	O	S	Y	T
M	A	O	B	O	A	K	G	O	J	E	A	B	A	D
M	U	N	P	G	N	S	W	S	U	R	S	B	L	M
S	U	S	A	K	Z	X	Q	A	H	N	N	L	N	N
U	D	S	S	T	E	I	V	U	H	A	H	J	P	N
C	P	L	K	O	E	D	M	R	X	B	R	C	G	L
Y	H	O	P	R	P	E	Z	Q	U	O	K	K	A	I
G	M	T	G	W	A	O	G	R	E	G	A	N	A	T
O	L	H	X	Y	J	T	R	V	C	U	X	G	D	S

ARCTIC TERN
BASKING SHARK
BAT
CHIMIPANZEE
CHIPMUNK
DINOSAUR
EGRET
HAWK
LION
MANATEE
MANDRILL
MASTIFF
MUSKRAT
OPOSSUM
PANGOLIN
QUOKKA
SALMON
SLOTH
TANAGER

Puzzle #10

ANIMALS

K	V	B	Y	Y	P	L	E	F	F	A	R	I	G	M
M	X	P	X	S	V	R	A	U	G	A	J	T	M	Q
E	T	S	A	T	P	H	R	Z	I	F	G	O	N	N
A	S	L	T	O	E	Z	T	H	U	M	I	N	A	M
D	G	U	F	D	Z	H	T	C	C	A	A	R	O	O
C	N	R	C	B	H	W	R	C	Y	N	G	A	S	W
R	H	A	U	E	E	O	I	Y	E	T	E	O	Q	L
L	R	A	U	A	N	R	O	C	H	S	R	C	U	A
S	E	I	R	T	S	M	N	C	C	Q	N	C	I	R
G	P	O	G	P	I	A	K	A	R	U	V	I	T	K
G	T	O	P	W	S	L	R	J	R	I	Q	G	O	K
Y	I	E	N	A	D	E	U	T	W	D	S	U	L	Y
O	L	U	X	E	R	X	A	S	L	V	M	N	U	B
K	E	T	P	L	X	D	D	L	R	U	I	N	J	T
L	S	E	T	A	R	B	E	T	R	E	V	N	I	

EARTHWORM
GIANT SQUID
GIRAFFE
HARP SEAL
HEN
IMAGO
INSECT
INVERTEBRATES
JAGUAR
LEOPARD
MEADOWLARK
MOSQUITO
NAUTILUS
ONAGER
REPTILE
ST. BERNARD
ULTRASAURUS
XENOPS

Coloring Pages - Inspirational

Quotes

always
STAY
HUMBLE
AND kind

DON'T LET
yesterday
TAKE UP
TOO MUCH
of today

DREAM IT
wish it
DO IT

EVERY
EXIT
IS AN
ENTRY
SOMEWHERE
ELSE

FAIL FAST
fail often
NEVER
GIVE UP
AND YOU WILL FIND
SUCCESS

GREAT
THINGS
never come
FROM
comfort
ZONES

important kind
fearless
I AM
strong
brave
worthy
blessed
capable
loved

WORTHY·KIND·STRONG·IMPORTANT·BRAVE·CAPABLE·LOVED·
I am

IF THE STARS
were made
TO WORSHIP
so will I

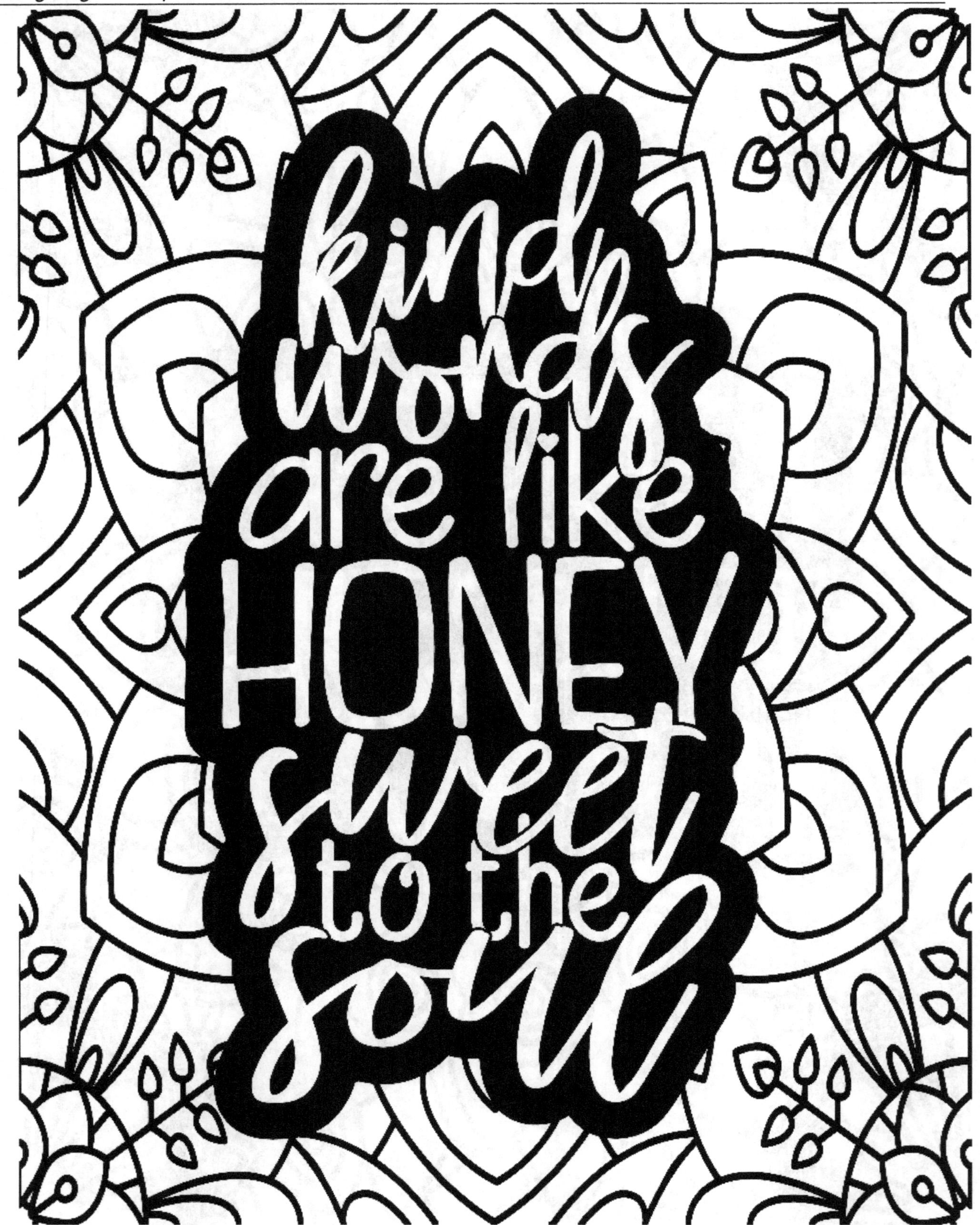
kind
words
are like
HONEY
sweet
to the
soul

LAUGH
loudly
LOVE
others
DREAM
big

BEGIN
each day
WITH A
grateful
heart

Stars CAN'T
Shine
WITHOUT
darkness

the SECRET
OF getting
AHEAD
IS GETTING
STARTED

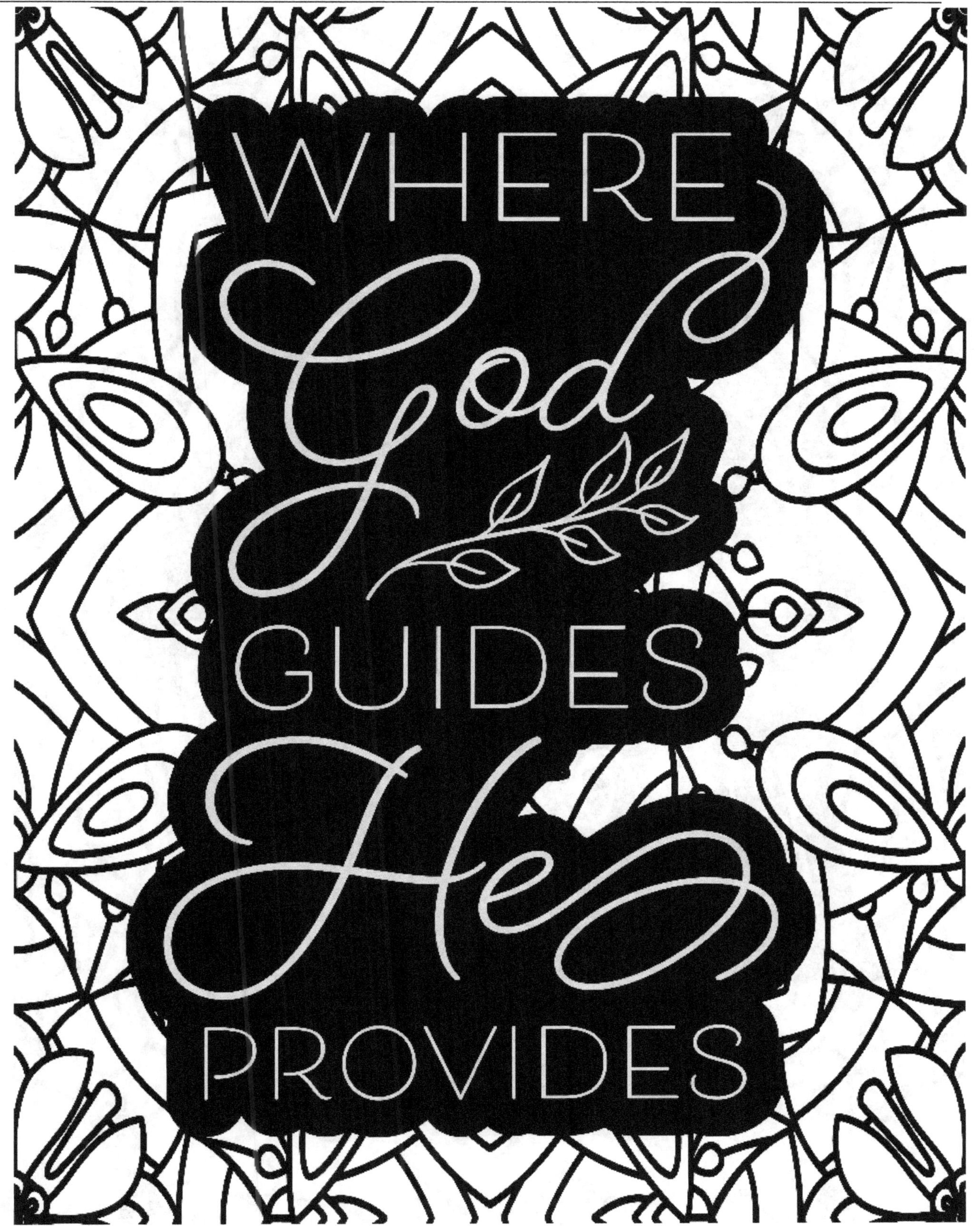
WHERE
God
GUIDES
He
PROVIDES

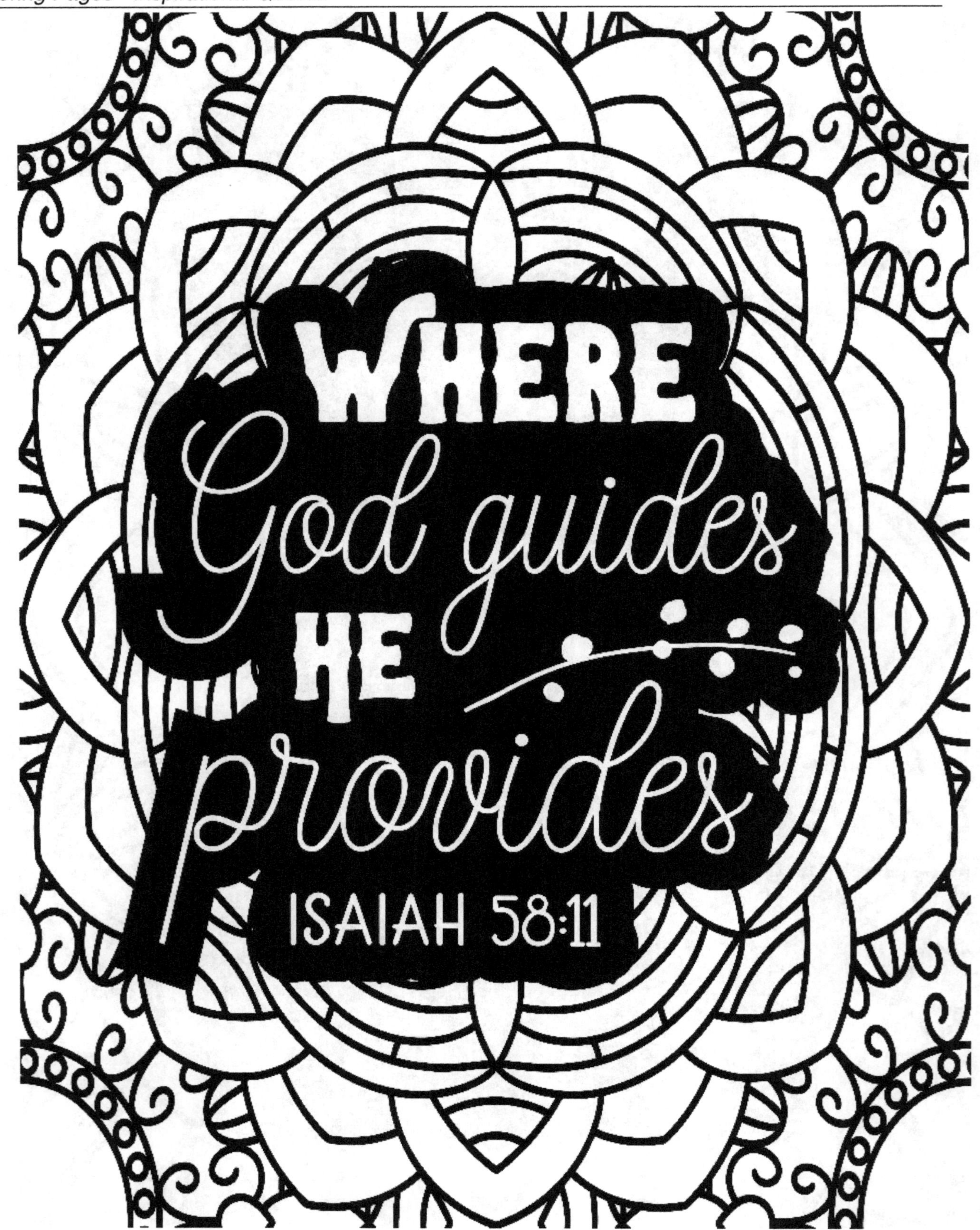
WHERE
God guides
HE
provides
ISAIAH 58:11

WITH GOD
all things
ARE POSSIBLE

Sudoku Solutions

Solution 1

2	5	6	4	9	3	7	1	8
9	4	8	7	1	6	5	2	3
1	7	3	8	5	2	4	6	9
7	8	2	3	6	4	9	5	1
3	6	1	5	8	9	2	4	7
4	9	5	1	2	7	8	3	6
8	2	4	6	7	1	3	9	5
5	1	9	2	3	8	6	7	4
6	3	7	9	4	5	1	8	2

Solution 2

9	3	1	8	6	2	7	4	5
4	5	7	3	1	9	8	6	2
8	6	2	5	4	7	9	1	3
7	2	4	1	5	6	3	9	8
3	1	6	7	9	8	5	2	4
5	8	9	4	2	3	6	7	1
2	9	8	6	3	1	4	5	7
6	7	5	2	8	4	1	3	9
1	4	3	9	7	5	2	8	6

Solution 3

2	5	3	1	4	8	6	7	9
7	6	9	3	2	5	1	4	8
4	8	1	9	6	7	5	2	3
3	1	4	2	5	9	7	8	6
5	2	7	8	3	6	9	1	4
6	9	8	4	7	1	2	3	5
1	4	5	7	9	3	8	6	2
8	3	6	5	1	2	4	9	7
9	7	2	6	8	4	3	5	1

Solution 4

3	8	1	4	5	9	2	6	7
5	2	9	6	1	7	4	3	8
4	7	6	2	8	3	5	1	9
7	3	5	1	9	2	6	8	4
8	6	2	3	4	5	7	9	1
9	1	4	8	7	6	3	2	5
6	5	7	9	2	1	8	4	3
1	4	3	5	6	8	9	7	2
2	9	8	7	3	4	1	5	6

Solution 5

5	7	4	2	1	8	3	9	6
1	6	3	9	5	7	8	2	4
9	8	2	6	3	4	7	5	1
7	1	9	3	4	6	2	8	5
2	4	5	1	8	9	6	7	3
8	3	6	7	2	5	1	4	9
3	5	7	4	6	2	9	1	8
4	2	1	8	9	3	5	6	7
6	9	8	5	7	1	4	3	2

Solution 6

9	4	2	3	5	1	7	6	8
5	6	7	4	2	8	9	3	1
1	3	8	7	6	9	5	2	4
4	2	3	1	8	5	6	9	7
6	1	9	2	3	7	4	8	5
8	7	5	6	9	4	2	1	3
7	8	6	5	1	2	3	4	9
2	9	4	8	7	3	1	5	6
3	5	1	9	4	6	8	7	2

Solution 7

2	8	7	3	4	6	9	5	1
6	4	3	9	1	5	2	7	8
5	9	1	8	2	7	4	3	6
1	7	2	6	9	8	5	4	3
3	5	4	1	7	2	6	8	9
8	6	9	5	3	4	7	1	2
9	3	6	4	5	1	8	2	7
7	1	5	2	8	9	3	6	4
4	2	8	7	6	3	1	9	5

Solution 8

2	1	4	3	6	9	5	8	7
3	9	7	8	2	5	1	6	4
6	5	8	1	7	4	3	2	9
8	4	9	7	5	2	6	1	3
5	3	6	4	1	8	7	9	2
1	7	2	6	9	3	4	5	8
4	2	5	9	3	1	8	7	6
7	8	1	2	4	6	9	3	5
9	6	3	5	8	7	2	4	1

Solution 9

2	5	1	8	7	4	9	6	3
7	4	9	1	6	3	8	5	2
3	6	8	2	5	9	4	1	7
4	3	2	9	8	1	6	7	5
8	9	7	5	3	6	1	2	4
5	1	6	7	4	2	3	9	8
1	7	3	6	2	8	5	4	9
6	8	5	4	9	7	2	3	1
9	2	4	3	1	5	7	8	6

Solution 10

3	5	1	8	4	9	7	6	2
2	7	4	3	1	6	8	5	9
8	6	9	5	7	2	1	4	3
1	4	8	7	5	3	2	9	6
9	2	7	6	8	4	5	3	1
6	3	5	2	9	1	4	7	8
4	9	3	1	2	5	6	8	7
7	1	6	4	3	8	9	2	5
5	8	2	9	6	7	3	1	4

Solution 11

6	4	2	5	9	7	1	3	8
8	5	1	6	4	3	2	7	9
3	9	7	1	8	2	6	4	5
7	8	6	2	5	4	3	9	1
4	3	5	7	1	9	8	6	2
1	2	9	3	6	8	4	5	7
2	7	4	8	3	5	9	1	6
5	6	3	9	2	1	7	8	4
9	1	8	4	7	6	5	2	3

Solution 12

1	8	7	5	6	2	9	3	4
3	6	5	9	8	4	2	1	7
9	4	2	3	7	1	6	5	8
4	7	9	2	1	3	8	6	5
8	1	3	6	5	7	4	9	2
5	2	6	4	9	8	3	7	1
2	9	1	7	4	6	5	8	3
7	5	4	8	3	9	1	2	6
6	3	8	1	2	5	7	4	9

Solution 13

2	3	5	6	7	8	9	1	4
6	1	7	5	9	4	2	8	3
9	4	8	3	2	1	6	7	5
5	9	3	8	4	2	7	6	1
8	2	6	1	5	7	3	4	9
1	7	4	9	3	6	5	2	8
7	6	9	4	1	3	8	5	2
4	5	2	7	8	9	1	3	6
3	8	1	2	6	5	4	9	7

Solution 14

4	9	1	2	6	3	5	7	8
2	6	5	8	7	1	4	9	3
7	8	3	5	9	4	2	6	1
8	3	9	6	5	2	1	4	7
5	7	4	3	1	9	6	8	2
1	2	6	4	8	7	3	5	9
3	1	7	9	4	5	8	2	6
6	5	2	7	3	8	9	1	4
9	4	8	1	2	6	7	3	5

Solution 15

6	1	2	3	7	4	8	9	5
4	7	5	2	9	8	1	6	3
3	9	8	6	5	1	2	4	7
9	2	6	4	1	7	3	5	8
7	3	1	8	6	5	9	2	4
5	8	4	9	2	3	7	1	6
2	6	3	5	8	9	4	7	1
8	5	7	1	4	2	6	3	9
1	4	9	7	3	6	5	8	2

Solution 16

8	1	7	9	5	2	6	3	4
5	3	4	1	8	6	9	7	2
6	2	9	7	3	4	5	8	1
3	6	5	2	7	8	1	4	9
9	4	1	5	6	3	7	2	8
2	7	8	4	1	9	3	5	6
4	9	3	6	2	7	8	1	5
1	8	2	3	9	5	4	6	7
7	5	6	8	4	1	2	9	3

Solution 17

3	5	1	9	2	6	4	8	7
8	2	4	1	7	3	5	6	9
7	9	6	4	8	5	2	3	1
1	3	2	6	4	7	8	9	5
6	4	5	2	9	8	7	1	3
9	8	7	3	5	1	6	4	2
2	1	9	5	6	4	3	7	8
5	6	8	7	3	9	1	2	4
4	7	3	8	1	2	9	5	6

Solution 18

1	2	4	7	3	8	9	5	6
8	5	7	9	4	6	2	3	1
9	3	6	2	5	1	7	8	4
3	7	5	1	8	9	6	4	2
2	8	1	6	7	4	3	9	5
6	4	9	3	2	5	1	7	8
5	9	3	4	6	2	8	1	7
7	6	8	5	1	3	4	2	9
4	1	2	8	9	7	5	6	3

Solution 19

6	5	7	4	3	2	9	1	8
9	4	2	7	1	8	6	5	3
3	1	8	5	9	6	4	2	7
7	3	4	2	6	5	8	9	1
2	8	6	1	7	9	5	3	4
1	9	5	3	8	4	2	7	6
4	6	3	9	2	7	1	8	5
5	7	9	8	4	1	3	6	2
8	2	1	6	5	3	7	4	9

Solution 20

5	1	2	7	4	3	8	6	9
3	9	6	5	8	2	4	1	7
7	4	8	6	1	9	3	2	5
8	5	1	4	9	7	6	3	2
9	6	3	2	5	1	7	4	8
2	7	4	8	3	6	9	5	1
6	3	5	9	2	8	1	7	4
4	8	7	1	6	5	2	9	3
1	2	9	3	7	4	5	8	6

Solution 21

7	3	1	5	8	4	2	6	9
5	6	4	7	9	2	3	1	8
8	9	2	1	3	6	5	7	4
2	8	9	6	4	7	1	3	5
6	5	3	2	1	8	9	4	7
4	1	7	3	5	9	6	8	2
3	4	6	9	7	5	8	2	1
1	7	5	8	2	3	4	9	6
9	2	8	4	6	1	7	5	3

Solution 22

2	8	9	7	6	4	3	5	1
6	5	7	2	3	1	4	9	8
3	1	4	8	5	9	6	7	2
9	3	6	5	4	8	2	1	7
8	4	2	9	1	7	5	3	6
1	7	5	3	2	6	8	4	9
7	2	3	6	9	5	1	8	4
5	9	1	4	8	2	7	6	3
4	6	8	1	7	3	9	2	5

Solution 23

4	1	8	2	5	3	9	7	6
3	6	7	1	4	9	5	2	8
2	9	5	8	6	7	3	4	1
7	3	6	5	9	4	8	1	2
9	4	1	7	2	8	6	5	3
8	5	2	6	3	1	7	9	4
1	8	9	3	7	2	4	6	5
6	2	4	9	8	5	1	3	7
5	7	3	4	1	6	2	8	9

Solution 24

6	2	7	5	9	3	4	1	8
8	3	4	6	1	7	5	9	2
1	5	9	4	8	2	3	6	7
5	8	3	1	4	9	7	2	6
4	6	2	7	3	8	9	5	1
7	9	1	2	6	5	8	4	3
3	4	5	8	2	6	1	7	9
9	1	6	3	7	4	2	8	5
2	7	8	9	5	1	6	3	4

Solution 25

6	7	4	3	8	5	9	2	1
3	1	5	7	9	2	4	6	8
9	2	8	1	6	4	3	7	5
8	6	9	2	3	7	1	5	4
4	3	2	6	5	1	7	8	9
7	5	1	9	4	8	6	3	2
2	4	7	8	1	3	5	9	6
1	9	3	5	2	6	8	4	7
5	8	6	4	7	9	2	1	3

Solution 26

3	4	1	9	8	2	6	7	5
6	2	9	4	5	7	1	8	3
7	8	5	6	3	1	9	2	4
8	1	4	5	6	3	2	9	7
5	3	7	8	2	9	4	6	1
2	9	6	1	7	4	3	5	8
4	6	2	7	1	5	8	3	9
1	7	3	2	9	8	5	4	6
9	5	8	3	4	6	7	1	2

Solution 27

1	4	8	5	7	3	6	2	9
5	3	2	9	1	6	8	4	7
7	6	9	4	2	8	5	1	3
3	7	6	2	4	1	9	8	5
9	2	5	3	8	7	4	6	1
4	8	1	6	5	9	3	7	2
2	5	7	8	3	4	1	9	6
8	9	3	1	6	2	7	5	4
6	1	4	7	9	5	2	3	8

Solution 28

2	9	6	8	7	4	1	5	3
1	8	5	6	9	3	7	4	2
3	4	7	2	5	1	6	9	8
4	5	8	3	1	2	9	7	6
6	1	2	7	8	9	5	3	4
9	7	3	5	4	6	2	8	1
5	6	9	4	2	8	3	1	7
8	2	1	9	3	7	4	6	5
7	3	4	1	6	5	8	2	9

Solution 29

4	6	9	5	7	8	2	3	1
7	3	5	4	1	2	9	6	8
2	1	8	6	3	9	5	4	7
1	7	2	3	4	5	8	9	6
3	5	6	9	8	1	7	2	4
8	9	4	7	2	6	1	5	3
9	4	3	8	5	7	6	1	2
5	2	7	1	6	3	4	8	9
6	8	1	2	9	4	3	7	5

Solution 30

4	9	2	8	3	7	6	1	5
1	3	5	4	2	6	8	7	9
8	7	6	5	1	9	4	3	2
2	4	1	6	8	5	7	9	3
7	5	8	2	9	3	1	6	4
3	6	9	1	7	4	2	5	8
5	2	3	7	4	1	9	8	6
6	1	4	9	5	8	3	2	7
9	8	7	3	6	2	5	4	1

Maze Solutions

Solution 1

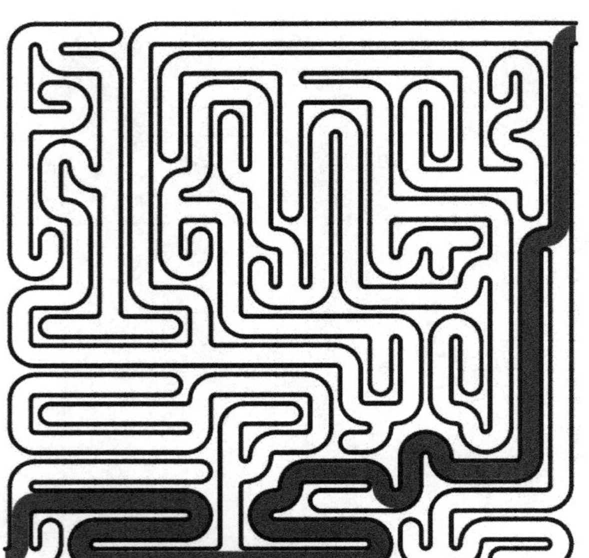

Solution 2

Solution 3

Solution 4

Solution 5

Solution 6

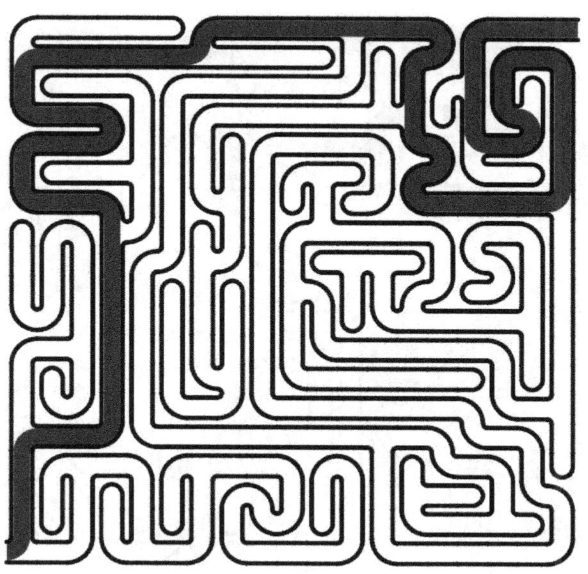

Solution 7

Solution 8

Solution 9

Solution 10

Solution 11

Solution 12

Solution 13

Solution 14

Solution 15

Solution 16

Solution 17

Solution 18

Solution 19

Solution 20

Solution 21

Solution 22

Solution 23

Solution 24

Solution 25

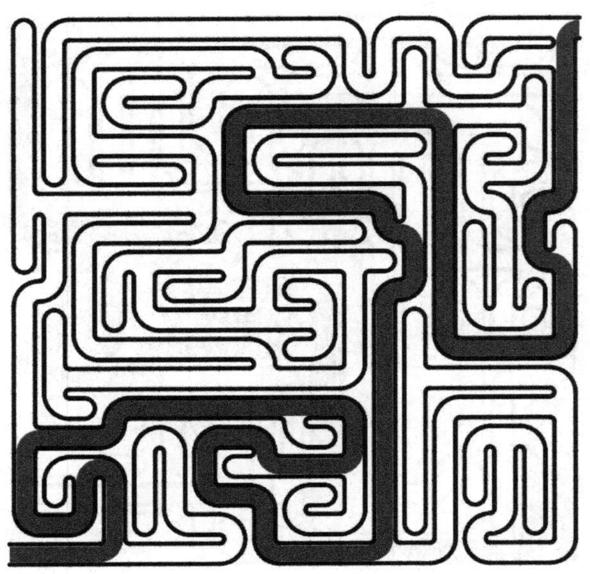

Solution 26

Solution 27

Solution 28

Solution 29

Solution 30

Word Scramble Solutions

Word Scramble List 1

SPECIAL

YULE

APPEARANCE

COLLAR

HILLS

SANTA

TOWN

ELM

REJOICE

TIPTOE

Word Scramble List 2

YULE

APPEARANCE

COLLAR

HILLS

SANTA

TOWN

ELM

REJOICE

TIPTOE

DECOR

Word Scramble List 3

APPEARANCE

COLLAR

HILLS

SANTA

TOWN

ELM

REJOICE

TIPTOE

DECOR

OVERCOAT

Word Scramble List 4

COLLAR

HILLS

SANTA

TOWN

ELM

REJOICE

TIPTOE

DECOR

OVERCOAT

NOSE

Word Scramble List 5

HILLS

SANTA

TOWN

ELM

REJOICE

TIPTOE

DECOR

OVERCOAT

NOSE

PINECONE

Word Scramble List 6

SANTA

TOWN

ELM

REJOICE

TIPTOE

DECOR

OVERCOAT

NOSE

PINECONE

STUFFER

Word Scramble List 7

TOWN

ELM

REJOICE

TIPTOE

DECOR

OVERCOAT

NOSE

PINECONE

STUFFER

YULETIDE

Word Scramble List 8

ELM

REJOICE

TIPTOE

DECOR

OVERCOAT

NOSE

PINECONE

STUFFER

YULETIDE

COCOA

Word Scramble List 9

REJOICE

TIPTOE

DECOR

OVERCOAT

NOSE

PINECONE

STUFFER

YULETIDE

COCOA

SAVIOR

Word Scramble List 10

TIPTOE

DECOR

OVERCOAT

NOSE

PINECONE

STUFFER

YULETIDE

COCOA

SAVIOR

DELICIOUS

Word Scramble List 11

DECOR

OVERCOAT

NOSE

PINECONE

STUFFER

YULETIDE

COCOA

SAVIOR

DELICIOUS

REDEEMER

Word Scramble List 12

OVERCOAT

NOSE

PINECONE

STUFFER

YULETIDE

COCOA

SAVIOR

DELICIOUS

REDEEMER

POLE

Word Scramble List 13

NOSE

PINECONE

STUFFER

YULETIDE

COCOA

SAVIOR

DELICIOUS

REDEEMER

POLE

GIFT

Word Scramble List 14

PINECONE

STUFFER

YULETIDE

COCOA

SAVIOR

DELICIOUS

REDEEMER

POLE

GIFT

BOOTS

Word Scramble List 15

STUFFER

YULETIDE

COCOA

SAVIOR

DELICIOUS

REDEEMER

POLE

GIFT

BOOTS

SILVER

Word Scramble List 16

YULETIDE

COCOA

SAVIOR

DELICIOUS

REDEEMER

POLE

GIFT

BOOTS

SILVER

SACK

Word Scramble List 17

COCOA

SAVIOR

DELICIOUS

REDEEMER

POLE

GIFT

BOOTS

SILVER

SACK

GIVE

Word Scramble List 18

SAVIOR

DELICIOUS

REDEEMER

POLE

GIFT

BOOTS

SILVER

SACK

GIVE

FRAME

Word Scramble List 19

DELICIOUS

REDEEMER

POLE

GIFT

BOOTS

SILVER

SACK

GIVE

FRAME

AFRAID

Word Scramble List 20

REDEEMER

POLE

GIFT

BOOTS

SILVER

SACK

GIVE

FRAME

AFRAID

CRECHE

Word Scramble List 21

POLE

GIFT

BOOTS

SILVER

SACK

GIVE

FRAME

AFRAID

CRECHE

FRUITCAKE

Word Scramble List 22

GIFT

BOOTS

SILVER

SACK

GIVE

FRAME

AFRAID

CRECHE

FRUITCAKE

FLATBREAD

Word Scramble List 23

BOOTS

SILVER

SACK

GIVE

FRAME

AFRAID

CRECHE

FRUITCAKE

FLATBREAD

SOCK

Word Scramble List 24

SILVER

SACK

GIVE

FRAME

AFRAID

CRECHE

FRUITCAKE

FLATBREAD

SOCK

RELIGIOUS

Word Scramble List 25

SACK

GIVE

FRAME

AFRAID

CRECHE

FRUITCAKE

FLATBREAD

SOCK

RELIGIOUS

SOUND

Word Scramble List 26

GIVE

FRAME

AFRAID

CRECHE

FRUITCAKE

FLATBREAD

SOCK

RELIGIOUS

SOUND

SERVICE

Word Scramble List 27

FRAME

AFRAID

CRECHE

FRUITCAKE

FLATBREAD

SOCK

RELIGIOUS

SOUND

SERVICE

REJOICING

Word Scramble List 28

AFRAID

CRECHE

FRUITCAKE

FLATBREAD

SOCK

RELIGIOUS

SOUND

SERVICE

REJOICING

BELONGING

Word Scramble List 29

CRECHE

FRUITCAKE

FLATBREAD

SOCK

RELIGIOUS

SOUND

SERVICE

REJOICING

BELONGING

EXCITEMENT

Word Scramble List 30

FRUITCAKE

FLATBREAD

SOCK

RELIGIOUS

SOUND

SERVICE

REJOICING

BELONGING

EXCITEMENT

SOUL

Colortile Solutions

1

2

3

4

5

6

7

8

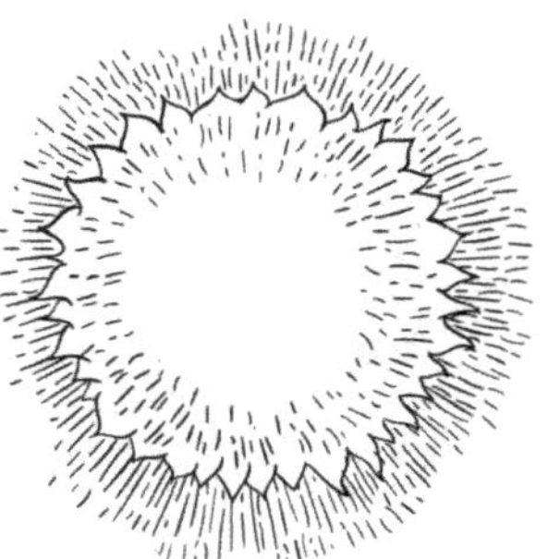

9

10

11

12

13

14

15

Word Search Solutions

COLUMBUS
Puzzle # 1

N	G	N	I	L	L	I	K		S	A	L	M	O	N
A				E	K	R	E	S	I	L	I	E	N	T
V			L	D	V	C	T	S	E	N	H			
I				U	E	I	A				A			
G				T	C	C	T	T			B			
A				Y		K	L	C	D		I			
T	R	Y	T			B	Y	A	U	R	T		F	
E	I	S	R	E	G	N	A	D	R	R	A		O	
	V		W	E	K	A	O	H	E	A	T	H	R	
	E			O	V	S	L	I	A	G	T	S	G	
	R				R	O	U	L	N	M	G	I	E	
	B					K	C	M	E	U	A	U	O	D
N	A	T	I	O	N	A	L	S		Y		S	R	N
	N					I	N	C	I	D	E	N	T	
	K			E	C	N	A	R	U	D	N	E		

GARDENING
Puzzle # 2

		E	F		S			C						T
	E		R	U	R	L			U	S	H	E	A	R
		P		U	M	A	A			L				U
H			O		T	I	R	T			T		H	N
O		T	C	R	N	L	G	E	E		R	U	A	K
R	Q	O	N	H	T	O	U	A		P	O		R	W
T	U	R		E	O	O	I	C	T		C		M	E
I	A	I	N		M	I	I	T	I	I	K		O	T
C	N	G		U	G	N	C	L	C	R	O		N	L
U	T	I			R		O	E	E	E	G	N	I	A
L	I	N			O	S		R		H	L	A	O	N
T	T	A			W		E		I		T	E	U	D
U	Y	L		N	E	P	O	R		V		O	S	S
R	E	N	E	D	R	A	G		Y		N		L	
E			H	A	N	G	I	N	G			E		C

THANKSGIVING
Puzzle # 3

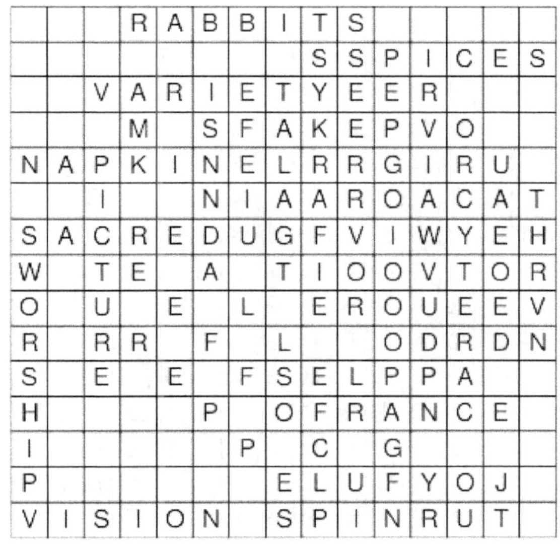

			R	A	B	B	I	T	S					
								S	S	P	I	C	E	S
		V	A	R	I	E	T	Y	E	E	R			
			M		S	F	A	K	E	P	V	O		
N	A	P	K	I	N	E	L	R	R	G	I	R	U	
		I			N	I	A	A	R	O	A	C	A	T
S	A	C	R	E	D	U	G	F	V	I	W	Y	E	H
W		T	E		A		T	I	O	O	V	T	O	R
O		U		E		L		E	R	O	U	E	E	V
R		R	R		F		L			O	D	R	D	N
S		E		E		F	S	E	L	P	P	A		
H					P		O	F	R	A	N	C	E	
I						P		C		G				
P							E	L	U	F	Y	O	J	
V	I	S	I	O	N		S	P	I	N	R	U	T	

FRUITS
Puzzle # 4

	S	U	O	I	C	I	L	E	D					G
	C					E	R	O	O	M				R
N	A	A				E	P	A	R	G	A	E	S	A
Y	O	Y	I	E	N	I	R	A	D	N	A	M		N
	R	L	O	M				G	R	A	N	A	D	A
P		R	E	M	I	C	A	C	O	G		M		D
L	O	C	E	M	I	T	B	I	L	I	M	B	I	I
A	P	L	E	B	Y	R	O					A	Y	L
N	U		E	M	D	R	E	L				R	A	L
T	L			M	P	U	A	H	L			E	N	A
A	A				O	E	O	N	C	O		L	G	
I	S					P	D	L	A		P	L	M	
N	A	Z	E	M	E	T	Z	A	C	C		A	E	
S	N			N	O	L	E	M	K	S	U	M	I	
	M	I	R	A	C	L	E	F	R	U	I	T		

HALLOWEEN
Puzzle # 5

		S	L	L	A	B	E	Y	E					
				I				L	L					
H	S	I	L	I	V	E	D		U	T				
				U		E	Y	G	H	O	S	T	L	Y
F	F				F			E			H	A		
R	L	L	A	F		D			P			G	H	
I	A			F	L	R	A	G		A		F		G
G	S			R	F	E		E			T	A		
H	H			I	R	S		N	R		F	C		
T	L			G	I	S		I		D		E	H	G
E	I			H	G	U		E				P	A	O
N	G	O	F	T	H	P			Y	R	I	A	F	R
I	H		R	E	T	H	G	I	F	E	R	I	F	Y
N	T			N						S	G	N	A	F
G			H	S	I	L	U	O	H	G		T		

GARDENING
Puzzle # 6

M		W			H		R	E	S	O	U	R	C	E
	H	I				Y					C		R	P
	S	T		A	B		B				U	F	E	L
	H	H	Y		R	O	O	R			T	R	S	A
C	R	E		H		R	T		I		T	A	I	N
S	U	R			R		A	A		D	I	G	S	T
I	B	L	I	O	S		N	N	N		N	R	T	I
M			T				I		G	I	G	A	A	N
P		E	N	I	V		C	R		E	S	N	N	G
L					V		A		E		M	T	C	S
I						A	L			D		E	E	
C	U	L	T	I	V	A	T	I	O	N	R		N	
I	Y	R	A	T	N	E	M	E	L	P	M	O	C	T
T				G	N	I	G	G	I	D			B	
Y					I	M	P	A	T	I	E	N	T	S

VALENTINES
Puzzle # 7

				T	G	N	I	N	E	T	S	I	L	
	E	T	A	M	H	C	U	P	C	A	K	E		
			T	B		G			L	I	E	V		T
	R		T		U		I		E			C		U
J	E	W	E	L	S	D		L	V	Y		O		X
	L		N				G		E		P	M		E
	A		D	I	P	U	C	E	R	L		P		D
S	T		A	F	F	I	N	I	T	Y	D	A	A	O
E	I	D	N	A	L	R	A	G			I	N		H
R	V		C								N	I	A	
E	E	S	E	I	L	I	O	D	D		N	O		C
N	S	A	R	R	O	W				E	E	N		
I	O	F	F	I	C	I	A	L	S	I	R	A	P	
T					R	E	T	T	E	L	E	V	O	L
Y		Y	S	A	R	C	N	Y	S	O	I	D	I	

THANKSGIVING
Puzzle # 8

		S					R	G						R
	S		Y			E	Z	E	E	R	F			E
		K		M		H		R	H	L				L
		G	N	Y	B		E	M		T	B			I
			N	A	T	O		A			A	B		S
	S	C		I	H	N	L	N	R			G	O	H
H	L	I	R	E	T	T	U	B		T				G
	C	E	S	O	F	A	V	O	U	R	H			T
		R	A	T	W	S	E		B					U
O	T	O	A	D	E	D	E	S	S					R
	T	S	L	E	E	R	S	V	T	T				K
		A	E	I	S	R			A	A	E			E
		E	T	I	V	N	I			E	E	E		Y
				O	R	E					L	R	W	
					P	P	S	Y	T	A	E	R	T	S

ANIMALS
Puzzle # 9

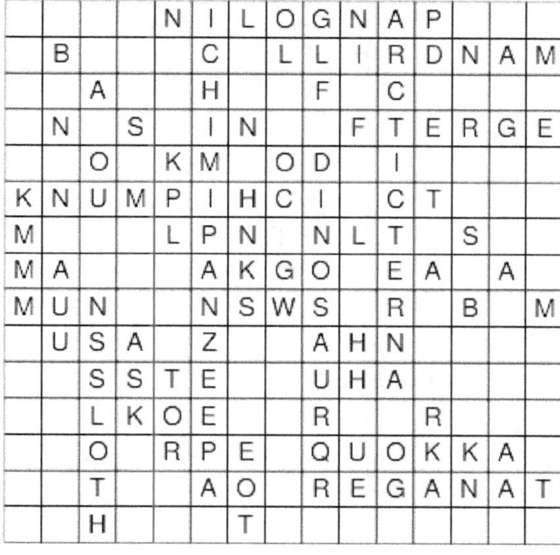

				N	I	L	O	G	N	A	P			
	B				C		L	L	I	R	D	N	A	M
		A			H			F		C				
	N		S		I	N			F	T	E	R	G	E
		O		K	M		O	D		I				
K	N	U	M	P	I	H	C	I		C	T			
M				L	P	N		N	L	T		S		
M	A				A	K	G	O		E	A		A	
M	U	N			N	S	W	S		R		B		M
	U	S	A		Z			A	H	N				
		S	S	T	E			U	H	A				
		L	K	O	E			R			R			
		O		R	P	E		Q	U	O	K	K	A	
		T			A	O		R	E	G	A	N	A	T
		H				T								

ANIMALS
Puzzle # 10

							E	F	F	A	R	I	G	
M						R	A	U	G	A	J			
E		S					R		I		G	O		
A	S		T				T			M	I	N		M
D		U				H	T			A	A		O	O
	N	R		B	H	W		C		N	G		S	W
	H	A	U		E	O			E	T	E	O	Q	L
L	R	A	U	A	N	R				S	R		U	A
S	E		R	T	S	M	N			Q	N		I	R
	P	O		P	I	A		A		U		I	T	K
	T	O	P		S	L	R		R	I			O	
	I		N	A		E	U	T		D				
	L			E	R		A	S	L					
	E				X	D		L		U				
	S	E	T	A	R	B	E	T	R	E	V	N	I	

THANKSGIVING
Puzzle # 11

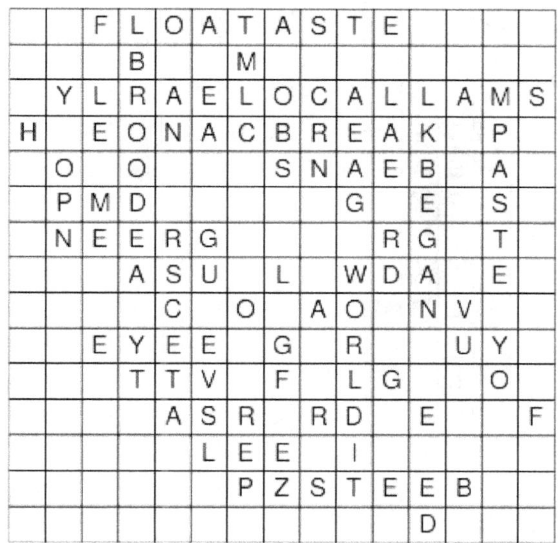

		F	L	O	A	T	A	S	T	E				
			B			M								
	Y	L	R	A	E	L	O	C	A	L	L	A	M	S
H		E	O	N	A	C	B	R	E	A	K		P	
	O		O				S	N	A	E	B		A	
	P	M	D						G		E		S	
	N	E	E	R	G					R	G		T	
			A	S	U		L		W	D	A		E	
				C		O		A	O		N	V		
		E	Y	E	E		G		R			U	Y	
			T	T	V		F		L	G			O	
				A	S	R		R	D		E			F
					L	E	E		I					
						P	Z	S	T	E	E	B		
											D			

CHRISTMAS
Puzzle # 12

E					S	U	R	P	R	I	S	E	S	
	V	F				A	L	L	E	R	B	M	U	
T	H	E	M	E		F	G	N	I	K	C	O	T	S
		S	N			F	A	M	O	U	S			
P		T		T				L	S	T	I	C	K	S
G	R	O	E				Y	U	L	E	T	I	D	E
L		O		C			B		E	I		O		
O	A	N	P		A			E	D		N		R	
R		U		H	L	E	N	N	A	L	F	G		G
I			N		E		P	I	E	R				
O				N		T		E	K	M	D			
U		P	O	L	A	R	S		C	P	E	E		
S	H	O	C	K						N	M	S	D	
	T	S	U	R	T						A	U	I	
		D	E	P	P	A	R	W				D	P	W

CHRISTMAS
Puzzle # 13

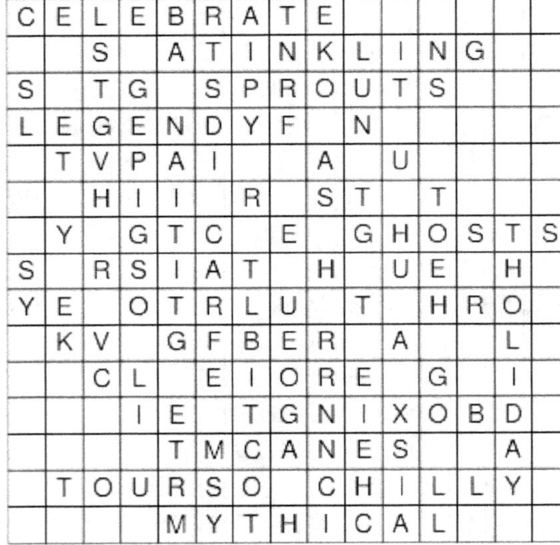

C	E	L	E	B	R	A	T	E						
		S		A	T	I	N	K	L	I	N	G		
S		T	G		S	P	R	O	U	T	S			
L	E	G	E	N	D	Y	F		N					
	T	V	P	A	I			A		U				
		H	I	I		R		S	T		T			
	Y		G	T	C		E		G	H	O	S	T	S
S		R	S	I	A	T		H		U	E		H	
Y	E		O	T	R	L	U		T		H	R	O	
	K	V		G	F	B	E	R		A			L	
		C	L		E	I	O	R	E		G		I	
			I	E		T	G	N	I	X	O	B	D	
				T	M	C	A	N	E	S			A	
	T	O	U	R	S	O		C	H	I	L	L	Y	
				M	Y	T	H	I	C	A	L			

ANIMALS
Puzzle # 14

			D		S	H	E	E	P					
			I	W	E	E	V	I	L					
		N	A	E	C	A	T	S	U	R	C			
			T		L	U	N	A	M	O	T	H		
			O	F	L	O	W	A	R	D	N	U	T	
R			M			B		C					N	
I						U	D	O	R	Y				A
V			K			F		C						
E			A		C	F		K						
R		X	N	Y	L	A		R						
O			G	U	L	L	N	O						
T			A			O	T	A	R	S	I	E	R	
T			R					C	R	H	U	S	K	Y
E		W	O	C	A	E	S	H		Y				
R		L	O	B	S	T	E	R						

COLUMBUS
Puzzle # 15

U	N	O	I	T	A	L	O	S	I					R
N				M	Y	R	A	T	I	N	A	S		E
I					M									C
V				D		U								O
E	C	I	T	I	Z	E	N	S	H	I	P			V
R		H		G	D		L	E	V	A	R	T		E
S			R	N		E	Y	A	N	T	H	E	M	R
A	T			I		R	F	D	Z		N			Y
L		F		T	S	O		E	R	O		A		
			I	Y		T	C	A	N	A	R	Y	R	
D	E	S	E	R	T	I	O	N		C	H	E		G
	W	O	U	N	D	S	S	P	I	C	E	S	S	
L	L	A	F	D	N	A	L		H			S		
E	G	A	Y	O	V				R	E	D	A	E	L
								C	A	R	R	A	C	K

THANKSGIVING
Puzzle # 16

	R					D	E	T	I	N	U			
	E	U	Q	I	N	U		T						
	A		O		L		G		R			O		
		D	B	V		E	N	R		U		N		
	E	D	A	R	A	P	V	O	O		G	I		
		G	K	N	E	S	G	A	S	U		O		
S			I	I	A	Y		E	R	A	P	N	Y	
	S		N	V	S	C	A		M	T	E	S		
	F	E	G	M	I	S		R		T	H	S		
	R		R	F	U	N	E		P	C	U			
	E	E		T	O	T	G	S		E	N	N		
	N		H		S	U	U			L	G			
	C			T	O	R	R	A	C	E	R			
	H	E	L	P	A	T	S	T		R	Y			
W	I	N	T	E	R	F			H	Y				

CPSIA information can be obtained
at www.ICGtesting.com
Printed in the USA
LVHW061147020123
736279LV00013B/850